Kit Carson

KIT CARSON

AND THE

WILD FRONTIER

by **RALPH MOODY**

Illustrated by **STANLEY W. GALLI**

RANDOM HOUSE · NEW YORK

Contents

Billy Coons

1

A Boy Worth One Cent

It has been said that great emergencies produce great men. It might almost seem that in 1809 destiny was preparing for the great crisis which the United States would face within the next generation. In that year two boys were born in the most humble of circumstances. Though they never met, these two boys, born in a state which seceded from the Union, were to be of tremendous importance in developing and holding that Union together. One of them would be a key figure in the expanding and securing of its frontier, and the other would be the rough-hewn genius who

would successfully guide it through its most perilous
years.

Abraham Lincoln was born in Hardin County, Kentucky, on February 12th, and Christopher Carson in
Madison County the following Christmas. Both boys
were the sons of ignorant, ne'er-do-well, frontiersman
fathers and uneducated, overworked, but highly reli-
gious mothers. Always poverty-stricken and dissatis-
fied with their surroundings, these two fathers kept
moving their large families farther and farther into
the unsettled wilderness of the West. Their only ambition for their sons was that they might grow up to
be strong, fearless, independent pioneers like themselves. As boys, both Abe and Kit were disappoint-
ments to their fathers.

It often happens that the thing we want most is the
one which seems most impossible for us to have. This
was true of both Abe Lincoln and Kit Carson. Abe
was tall and extremely strong, but he was not interested in being a frontiersman. From early boyhood,
his interest was in books and book learning. But there
was little possibility of gaining an education on the
American frontier. Kit had no interest in books or book
learning. From the time he could walk, he wanted to
be a giant frontiersman like his older brothers, but he
was the runt of all the fourteen Carson children.

It would seem hard to find two boys so entirely dif-

ferent. But they were alike in many ways although
Abe Lincoln attained a greatness far beyond that
reached by Kit Carson. Each lost one of his parents
in his early boyhood, and was raised in the home of a
stepparent. Neither boy was outstanding as a child;
both were inclined to be lazy in their early teens;
and each was slow to develop his full powers. But,
from early manhood, both gained the respect of those
who knew them, because of the same high qualities of
character—steadfastness of purpose, absolute honesty,
truthfulness, cool judgment in the face of seeming disaster, and an unshakable faith in God.

The Boones and the Carsons had been frontier
neighbors for two generations. Not long before Kit
was born, Daniel Boone had moved his family from
Kentucky into the wilds of Missouri. When Kit was
a year old, his father loaded his few sticks of furni-
ture, his wife, and younger children into an ox cart,
and headed west on the Boone Trail. He followed the
trail to its end and built a rough log cabin near the
banks of the Missouri River—the farthest west of any
American settlement. A few other cabins were scattered
there by the great river, and the settlement was called
Franklin.

The year 1822 had a great effect upon Franklin and
upon the life of Kit Carson. In that year Mexico won

her independence from Spain, and General Ashley organized and took into the Rockies the first American expedition of beaver trappers.

By the Louisiana Purchase, made in 1803, the United States had bought from France all the land lying between the Mississippi River and the Continental Divide in the Rocky Mountains. The southern boundary was considered to be the Rio Grande, but this was not clearly set forth in the treaty. When Spain disputed France's right to sell what is now Texas, New Mexico, and parts of Colorado and western Kansas, the United States had given up its claim to that territory. It was called New Mexico, and Santa Fe was its capital.

Eight hundred miles west of Franklin, where the southeast fringe of the Rockies reaches out into the plains and deserts, was the town of Santa Fe. It had been founded by the Spanish padres in 1605 and was built as the central mission in the midst of the centuries-old Pueblo Indian villages along the Rio Grande.

Before the Mexican revolution, Spain had permitted no foreign goods to be brought into her territory. Though the New Mexicans despised the *gringos,* they clamored for American merchandise. After winning their independence from Spain, they were willing to pay very high prices for it. By paying tribute of $500 a wagonload to the New Mexican governor, American merchants were permitted to bring caravans of goods

into Santa Fe. The profits were enormous. Most of
these goods were sent by boat up the Missouri River to
Franklin. There the merchandise was loaded onto
great eight-mule prairie schooners, and the caravans
rolled west over the newly blazed Santa Fe Trail.

In 1800 Beau Brummel had popularized the beaver
hat in England. By 1822 the rivers of England and the
eastern United States had been trapped clear of
beaver, but in the unknown streams of the Rocky
Mountains they abounded. Prime beaver pelts were
bringing six dollars apiece, and General Ashley was
to become fabulously wealthy from his trapping expeditions.

Beaver pelts were in prime condition only from October to May. From mid-December till the first of
April the beaver were safe in their lodges which were
frozen as hard as stone. The mountains were wild and
unmapped; Indians were always on the warpath
against the white men who were taking their game;
and the winters were severe. Only the hardiest and
strongest men could survive as trappers.

Every one of the hundred frontiersmen Ashley took
on his expedition of 1822 prided himself on his size,
strength and reckless courage. And they were all in
their early twenties. Among them were Jedediah Smith,
Jim Bridger, William Sublette and Thomas Fitzpatrick.
Along with Old Bill Williams, Jim Beckwourth and

Joe Walker, they became famous as the greatest of the mountain men. Following General Ashley's success, other trapping expeditions were made up, and many frontiersmen went to the mountains in pairs or small parties. Among them were the two oldest Carson boys, William and Big Mose, both giants of men.

With the Santa Fe trade and the outfitting of trappers, Franklin became the busiest settlement on the western frontier. Around its big central square there were trading posts, a blacksmith's forge and a saddler's shop. There was a meeting house and even a doctor. From the square, one trail led north along the river to Oregon Territory and the Northwest. Another led west to the ferry across the Missouri and on over the prairies to Santa Fe. Steamers were coming up the river from St. Louis, and pioneers were wearing the old Boone Trail into deep wagon ruts.

Kit Carson was now fifteen. A frontier boy of that age was supposed to be ready to do a man's work. But Kit showed little inclination to work and was barely five feet tall. His stepfather was disappointed and almost ashamed of the shy, towheaded, bandy-legged boy. There was no use trying to make a frontiersman out of such a backward little runt. All he would ever be good for was a job where size made no difference. So Kit was bound out to David Workman, the saddler, to serve a seven-year apprenticeship.

David Workman was a good saddler, a good teacher

and a hard worker. He expected his apprentice to be a hard worker and a good learner and to become an expert saddle and harness maker. Kit was nearly as disappointing to him as he had been to his stepfather. He had no trouble in learning, but he hated every hour he spent at his bench. His mind was seldom on his work.

All day long, through the isinglass window by his bench, Kit could see the big Conestoga wagons being pulled toward the ferry on their way to Santa Fe. Hunters, going to the prairies for buffalo, rode fractious horses through the square, and French Canadian voyageurs from the river stopped to fill their whiskey jugs at the Franklin still. Half-drunk Indians, spoiled by the white man's settlement, slumped against buildings, stole anything they could get their hands on, and traded it for more whiskey.

Mountain men, traders and trail-wagon drivers came to the saddler's shop to have their equipment repaired. But it was only the mountain men who set Kit's pioneer blood boiling. Great towering, raw-boned men, they came to Franklin with their bundles of beaver furs. Until the last penny from their catch had been spent, the settlement was in a turmoil. Drinking, dancing, shouting and boasting ruled the frontier. As Kit watched them and listened to their tales of narrow escapes, his eyes sparkled, the awl dropped from his fingers, and he forgot the saddle on the bench before him.

By the summer of 1826 Kit had served two years
of his apprenticeship. His arms and shoulders had developed, but he was still small, and he had become
round-shouldered from the hard work at the bench.
That summer the saddler's shop was swamped with
work. Charles Bent and Ceran St. Vrain were fitting
out a bigger wagon train than had ever taken the
Santa Fe Trail. There would be about thirty great
Conestoga wagons, each pulled by eight mules. Harness had to be made for the mules.

While the harness was in the making, Captain
Charles Bent came often to the saddler's shop. He was
a dark-haired, ruddy-faced young man, always dressed
in fringed doeskin, wide Mexican hat, and beaded
moccasins. He and David Workman often talked of
Santa Fe, of Taos—the little Mexican settlement that
the mountain men had adopted as their headquarters
—and of the Indian trading post that Bent and
St. Vrain planned to build on the Arkansas River.
Kit liked Captain Bent's quiet assurance and admired
him from the first day he saw him.

On the last day of August the final piece of harness
for the big caravan was finished. On the first day of
September Kit was missing from his bench in the
saddler's shop. Poor apprentice that he had been,
Kit was liked by David Workman who had a good
sense of humor. The next issue of the Franklin paper
carried this advertisement:

"NOTICE: TO WHOM IT MAY CONCERN: That Christopher Carson, a boy about sixteen years old, small for his age, but thickset, light hair, ran away from the subscriber, living in Franklin, Howard County, Mo., to whom he had been bound to learn the saddler's trade, on or about the first day of September. He is supposed to have made his way toward the upper part of the State. All persons are notified not to harbor, support, or subsist said boy under penalty of the law. One cent reward will be given to any person who will bring back the said boy. DAVID WORKMAN."

2

Wandering Runt of the Frontier

At dawn on the morning of September 1, 1826, the Bent-St. Vrain wagon train was stretched out for half a mile on the west bank of the Missouri. Half-broken mules were rearing and plunging in their harness; and rough, bearded teamsters were cursing and cracking the long lashes of their whips. Captain Charles Bent had just raised one foot to the step of his carriage. Close behind him, a quiet voice said, "Cap'n, suh, I come to hire out to ye to go to Santy Fee. I can mend up the saddles and harness as gits busted on the way."

The captain turned and recognized the bandy-

"Us Carsons ain't a-scared of nothin'," said the boy.

legged boy he had seen in the saddler's shop. He frowned a bit and said, "Sorry, Bub, but you're a little late. I've already got a . . ."

Kit tried his best to cover his disappointment, but Captain Bent saw it. He smiled and asked, "Can you ride?"

"Shorely."

"Afraid of Indians? There's a lot of bad ones out there."

Against his shoulder, Kit carried the old squirrel rifle that had been his father's. The long barrel reached three feet above his coonskin cap. He pushed it higher and said, "Us Carsons ain't a-scared of nothin'."

There was no bragging in the way Kit said it, and there was no wavering of his bright blue eyes from those of Charles Bent.

"Think you could herd the loose stock? We've got a mean bunch, and the job would only pay your keep. Where's your blanket?"

Kit didn't care what the job paid or how hard it was. With his free hand he pulled his linsey-woolsey jacket together across his chest. "Don't need no blanket," he said. "Got a warm coat. I'm right good at mindin' cavvy, Cap'n Bent."

Though the caravan had no need of extra help, and a youngster might become a nuisance, Captain Bent liked the courage and determination of the soft-spoken boy and took him along. Before Santa Fe was reached, the liking between the boy and man had turned to admiration. Later it became a friendship which lasted throughout the captain's life.

Kit's job was far from easy. There were more than a hundred loose animals in the cavvy—spare mules, saddle horses, mares with colts, and slow-footed beef cattle for butchering. From dawn until the animals were corralled in the wagon circle at sunset, Kit had to fight to keep the mixed cavvy bunched behind the wagon train that crept westward at about a mile an hour. As the country grew wilder and drier, men and animals suffered from thirst. The cavvy tried to spread in all directions, searching for water. Night guards had to be kept against marauding Indians and the gray prairie wolves that howled in the darkness beyond the picketed wagon mules.

As the caravan neared the Arkansas River, the wolves pressed in closer, and the teamsters kept their rifles loaded and close at hand. One wolf, bolder than the rest, made a rush for a straggling colt, and Andy Broadus grabbed for his rifle. The hammer jarred loose from its lock; the gun fired; and the bullet shattered Andy's arm below the elbow. The caravan stopped, and the men crowded around Andy. But Kit couldn't leave the cavvy. Captain Bent knew the arm would have to be amputated if Andy's life was to be saved. None of the men knew anything about surgery, and Broadus wouldn't let them experiment on him.

His arm was bound up, and he was put to ride in one
of the wagons.

Nearing Walnut Creek, the wagon train pulled into
camping formation long before sunset. Andy Broadus
was delirious. Gangrene had set into his arm; ugly
spots showed nearly to his shoulder; and in his delir-
ium he begged the men not to let him die. But the condition of the arm was so bad that none of them dared
try to amputate it. Wriggling through the crowd, Kit
looked up into Captain Bent's face earnestly, and said,
"Cap'n, suh, I kin do it. I seen the doctor in Franklin
do it onc't."

At first the men thought Kit was too young, but his
confidence in himself gave them confidence in him. The
operation was a success. For a day or two, as the caravan crept westward, Andy hung to life by a thread.
Two months later when Santa Fe was reached, he was
entirely recovered. The arm stub had healed perfectly.

Kit had an exceptionally photographic mind and a
keen sense of observation. Just as he had observed and
remembered exactly how the doctor had performed an
amputation, he had observed and remembered all he
had seen and heard on the Santa Fe Trail. His body
had toughened from the trip, and he had learned to
tighten his belt against the days of short rations and
thirst. But stretch as he might, his head still reached
barely to the top of a wagon wheel.

The crew was paid off at the end of the trip, and

Captain Bent did better by Kit than he had promised. He gave him a few Spanish dollars, his blanket, a horn of powder for his old squirrel rifle, and a bar of lead for bullets. Santa Fe held little interest for Kit. It was Taos, headquarters of the mountain men, that his mind was set on. A few of the scouts from the caravan were going there, and they took Kit along with them.

Just as they are today and were when Columbus discovered America, the two community houses of Taos Indian Pueblo stood on either side of Taos Creek in 1826. Behind them rose the San Juan range of the Rockies, and the little Mexican settlement of Taos was a few miles down the valley. It was only a dozen or so flat-roofed adobe cabins built around a trading post and a central plaza. When Kit and the scouts rode into Taos, it was mid-November. Winter had come to the Rockies; the fall trapping parties had long been gone into the mountains; and there was no work for an under-sized, bow-legged boy.

A few broken-down and drunken mountain men were hanging around Ewing Young's trading post. Among them Kit recognized Old Kincade. He had been one of the Carsons' neighbors in Franklin long before the Santa Fe Trail was opened. Years in the icy water of the beaver streams had crippled his body with rheumatism. And Taos lightning—the raw whiskey which he distilled for the mountain men—had nearly crippled his mind. He lived in a little hovel on the outskirts.

Kincade was an excellent gunsmith. When he was sober enough, he repaired guns for the mountain men. Barely able to make a living for himself, he took Kit in.

Kit's ability to make friends and his experience in the saddler's shop stood him in good stead that winter. He did odd jobs for Ewing Young, the owner of the trading post, and repaired saddles, harness and gear. From the Mexican women he learned to understand and speak Spanish, to tan buckskin, and to fashion it into coats and breeches. Watching Kincade, helping him repair guns, and listening to his endless stories of trapping, Indians, and the mountains, Kit learned much from the wise old man. "Rivers is the roads of the mountains," Kincade would tell him. "Ain't no two of 'em looks alike, runs alike, nor tastes alike. Never leave water till ye'd know it if ever ye seen it again. Never turn a bend or cross a ridge till ye look back and git the lay of the land wrote down in your head. Never trust an Injun when ye got ary thing he's likely to crave, and never trap a stream from the top down. Ain't a varmint smarter'n a beaver; he'll read sign of ye as the water fetches it down a-past him." When spring came, Old Kincade "went under." There would be no trappers going to the mountains till fall, and there was no way for Kit to make a living in Taos. He put his old flintlock over his shoulder and walked the eighty miles to Santa Fe to find a job.

There was no work for a *gringo* boy in Santa Fe. For two days Kit walked the streets with an empty stomach. Then, much as he hated to, he took a job herding cavvy in a caravan going back to Franklin. Nearing the Missouri River, the eastbound train met one heading for Santa Fe. Its leader needed a guide and interpreter, and Kit got the job.

Back in Santa Fe, Kit wasted no time. It was early October—time for the trapping expeditions to go into the mountains. With his blanket and squirrel rifle over his shoulder, he hit the trail up the Rio Grande for Taos, living on rabbits and prairie dogs he shot on the way.

Ewing Young's trading post was crowded with men when Kit reached Taos. The last trapping expedition of the fall was being made up. Any men not chosen would be left to starve through the winter in Taos. Pushing and crowding up toward the counter, those at the back shouted to the captain not to overlook them. Kit didn't want to be overlooked either and tried to wriggle his way through the press of mountaineers. A burly hand grabbed him by the coat collar. He was flung sprawling toward the door, and a rough voice shouted, "Git out'n here, Bub! Ye ain't big enough for weasel-trap bait!"

There was no use for Kit to stay in Taos; he could only starve. Again he walked the eighty miles to Santa Fe. That time he had better luck. He got a job at a dollar a day, driving team in a wagon train going down river to El Paso. The trip across the deserts took until late November, and there was no work to be found in El Paso. Taos had become home to Kit, and there was only one way to get there. He spent part of his pay for a wool coat, filled his powder horn, bought lead for bullets, and walked the four hundred miles over the *Jornado del Muerto*—the Journey of Death—to Taos.

It was Christmas Day, 1827, Kit's eighteenth birthday, when, half frozen, he pushed open the door of Ewing Young's trading post. "What ye doin' here, Bub, and how'd ye git here?" Captain Young shouted. "Heard tell ye was gone to El Paso del Norte. Set here by the fire whilst I fetch ye a bait of hot coffee."

"I was to del Norte, but I come home," Kit told him. "I'm eighteen now, Cap'n, and I reckon on bein' handy abouts when they pick the next trappin' outfits for the mountains."

"You forgit 'bout them mountains, Bub. Ye ain't never goin' to be sizable enough for trappin'. How'd ye git here from El Paso?"

"Walked. There wa'n't no other way to come."

"Who with?"

"Nobudy. Wa'n't nobudy comin' this-a-way."

"Wagh!" was all the Captain said for a few minutes, but in his mind he was seeing the winter desert between El Paso and Taos—Apache Indian country so dangerous that only the early Spanish padres had dared cross it alone. What a shame that a boy with this much courage should be such a little runt! Passing a steaming tin of strong black coffee to Kit, he asked, "How 'bout you bunkin' up with me for the winter and doin' the cookin'?"

Kit spent a good winter at Ewing Young's trading post. There was plenty to eat. He grew nearly two inches and learned a lot about beaver and the mountains from trappers who hung around the post. Though he was the favorite of Captain Young and the men, they ribbed him about thinking he could ever be a mountain man, and he wasn't happy. When spring came, he took his blanket and old squirrel rifle and set out for Santa Fe. He'd come back, but when he did he'd be ready for the mountains.

For the next year and a half, Kit took any job he could find where the work would be hard and where he'd have plenty to eat. There was just one determination in his mind; he was going to be a mountain man. What he lacked in size, he'd make up in strength and skill. He drove an eight-mule team over the Santa Fe Trail, and another six hundred miles south to Chihuahua in Old Mexico. He worked in the old Spanish copper mines on the divide between the Rio Grande and the Gila River. But always he was training himself to become a mountain man, toughening his body, breaking and riding wild horses, hunting wolves with the old squirrel rifle, and schooling himself to remember every trail he ever followed. As he lay in his blanket at night, he went over in his mind every Indian scrape he had heard the mountain men tell of during the winters in Taos and planned what he would have done if he'd been in the same scrape. By the fall of 1829 he had grown to five feet, seven inches and weighed a hundred and sixty pounds. His body was as tough as whang leather. He could rope and ride any wild horse on the prairies and could shoot the eye out of a racing jack rabbit. He quit the mines and again walked to Taos, three hundred miles to the north.

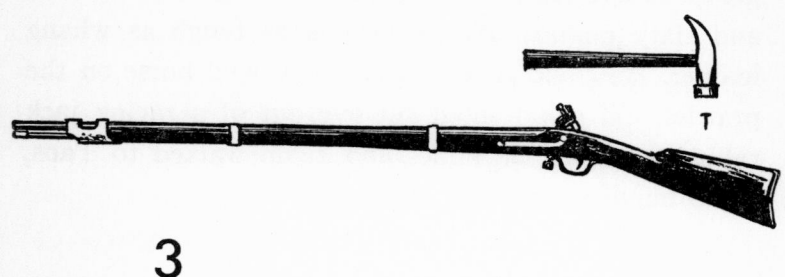

3

First Brass Tack

Americans were forbidden to trap in Mexican territory, but in the spring of 1829 Ewing Young had taken a party of trappers into the Mogollon Mountains, far to the southwest of Santa Fe. Their catch of beaver had been good, but on their way home they were attacked by Apache Indians. Their packs were stolen, and several men killed.

When Kit reached Taos, Captain Young was outfitting a party of forty men to go back into the Mogollons. The trip would be dangerous. After their success of the spring, the Apaches would be sure to attack. If captured by the Mexicans, the whole party might spend years in Mexican prisons. Because of the danger, Young was offering the men a share in the furs, but only seasoned Indian fighters were being chosen; most of them rough, tough French Canadians. Thirty-nine men had been chosen, and Kit was half smothered in the crowd when the Captain shouted, "Didn't I see that Carson young'un come in? Hey, Kit, come on up here!"

Kit pushed his way up to the counter, squared his shoulders, and said, "Howdy, Cap'n Young."

The Captain's eye was quick to see the change in Kit.

"Growed a mite, ain't ye?" he said. "Here tell ye been a-workin' down to the copper mines in the Mogollons."

"Yes, suh."

"Learn the lingo of any of them Injuns down that-a-way?"

"Yes, suh. I kin savvy mostly any of 'em."

"Might come in handy. Injun fightin' and beaver trappin' is powerful rough on a little man. Reckon ye could stand up to it?"

Kit had never been so happy, but he didn't let it show in his face, or move his eyes from those of Captain Young. "Ain't nothin' too rough if a man ain't scared," he answered. Then, because he couldn't write his name, Kit marked his X in the book where the

Captain wrote Kit Carson, and listed the equipment he would be furnished.

To mislead the government authorities into thinking he was going to trap in United States, rather than Mexican territory, Captain Young led his trapping party north from Taos. When well toward the boundary, he made a wide circle of nearly three hundred miles to the southwest, through the desolate Navajo Indian country. The first trapping camp was pitched on the headwaters of the Salt River, the northern tributary of the Gila, which rises near the present Arizona-New Mexico line.

It was here that the Apaches had defeated Captain Young's last trapping party, and preparations were made for another attack. It was not long in coming. Screeching and howling, the Indians rushed the camp from every direction with knives, lances, and tomahawks. Kit flung himself behind a saddle pack, and lay motionless, with the stock of his rifle pressed tight against his shoulder. Remembering Kincade's teaching, he held his fire until his rifle sights were trained on the chest of a charging warrior. Then he pressed the trigger, ducked low, and rammed another charge into the barrel.

The fight was short; the Indian weapons were no match for the trappers' rifles. Fifteen were killed, and the rest went dodging and running back into the hills.

The coolness Kit had shown in the fight with the

Apaches had caught Captain Young's eye. "Wagh!" he shouted when Kit was driving the first brass tack into the stock of his new rifle. "Might happen ye'll make a mountain man yet, lad." Next day Kit was put on the trap-line with Basil Lajeunesse, the most skillful French Canadian trapper in the party.

Captain Young trapped the Salt River and its tributaries to the lower end of what is now Roosevelt Reservoir. Then he turned north and trapped the Verde River for a hundred miles to its source near the present city of Flagstaff. This was probably the first American party to enter central Arizona. Beaver were plentiful, but the Indians pestered the trappers continually. They would sneak into camp at night to cut the throats of mules or to plunder packs, and would steal traps from the beaver ponds.

Fabulous stories of California had reached the American frontier. Though Captain Young had little idea of the distance, or of the deserts that lay between, he decided to go there and trap the waters of the Sacramento River. From the headwaters of the Verde, he sent twenty-two of his men back to Taos with what was left of the catch, choosing his eighteen best for the expedition to California. By this time Kit had proved himself to be so good a trapper and Indian fighter that the Captain chose him for the California band.

The Gila River formed the natural route from the

Rio Grande to California. It had been used by the Indians for centuries, and the remains of some of their oldest villages are in its valley. But this was not yet known to the American frontiersmen. Captain Young led his little party straight west, across an unexplored desert—one of the most rugged in the world. Both men and animals struggled against almost unbelievable hardships.

For four days no water or game was found, and only the scantest forage for the animals. Though it was early December, men's eyes burned with the wind-driven sand; their lips cracked and swelled from thirst. One after another, the starving mules fell in their tracks and died. As they collapsed, they were butchered and their stringy flesh was wolfed down by the starving men.

Late on the fourth day the remaining mules pricked up their ears, and the stronger of them staggered ahead at a weaving trot. Long before the green of a little canyon could be seen, they had smelled water. Here was grass for the animals, but no food for the men. A halt of two days was made, and a couple of the weaker mules were butchered. The men rested as the animals grazed and gained sufficient strength to go on.

At the end of another four waterless days, few of the mules were left. The men's eyes were sunk deep in their bony faces, and their purple tongues showed through shell-dry lips. Near sunset the mules again pricked up their ears and strained forward. The famished men staggered after them, knowing that water must be close ahead. This time it was a great river. They had reached the Colorado, near the southern tip of the present state of Nevada.

Mojave Indians were found farming along the river. They were friendly to the strange white men, brought them a fat horse for butchering, and traded corn and beans for knives and trinkets. For three days Captain Young and his men rested by the great river, while they and what animals they had left ate hungrily and regained strength.

For generations the Mojaves had traded for sea shells with the coast Indians and knew the country between. Through sign language, the trappers learned from them that the ocean lay two weeks' journey to the west. They were told of a river which rose in the mountains near the sea and ran upside down until it was lost in a desert. And the desert was so wide and barren that no man could cross it without carrying water.

Forewarned, Captain Young loaded his few remaining mules with water pouches, and the party again set off into trackless desert. With their scant ration of corn, beans and water, the men suffered less during the next three days than the animals, for which no provisions could be made. Still their hardship was almost unbearable. The wind-whipped sand cut into their faces and eyes. The midday sun glared on the salt-crusted flats. With no shelter, the nights were freezing cold.

At the end of the third day, the bed of the Mojave River was found, but it was bone dry. Following cloud-bursts, the Mojave is a raging torrent; but in the dry season its water runs deep below the desert sands. For two more days Captain Young and his eighteen trappers dragged themselves up the dry stream bed. One mule after another collapsed. The men gasped for breath through cracked lips and parched throats.

At the end of the fifth day after leaving the Colorado, water was reached in the Mojave River bed. It took four days for the exhausted party to reach the headwaters of the Mojave. It took another four to climb the range of mountains to the west. On Christmas, Kit's twentieth birthday, they dragged themselves over a low mountain pass and looked down into the green San Bernardino Valley of California.

On this expedition to California, Kit proved himself to be the equal of the best mountain men. He recovered from the hardships of the desert more quickly than most of the men. He showed courage, good judgment and leadership. After resting and re-equipping at Mission San Gabriel, Captain Young led his party northwest for nearly four hundred miles, trapping the

streams that flowed into the San Joaquin River from
the Sierras.

The California missions had been established by
Father Junipero Serra in the 1770s. The settlements
had been built around the missions; hundreds of Indians had been converted; large herds of horses and
cattle were kept; and a few Mexican soldiers were
billeted. The mission priests were powerful in the
Mexican government, and it would have been impossible for Americans to trap in California without their
good will.

On reaching Mission San Jose at the southern tip
of San Francisco Bay, Captain Young found the padre
very much upset. There had been a threatened rebellion of the converted Indians, and a party of them had
run away to join unfriendly Indians in the mountains.
Mexican soldiers from the mission had been sent to
bring them back. But they had been severely beaten,
and the priest appealed to Captain Young for help.
The Captain didn't dare risk the priest's displeasure.
Neither did he wish to risk his whole party on a wild-
goose chase into the mountains. He told Kit to take
a few men and make a show of trying to bring the
runaways back.

To Captain Young the expedition might have been
a wild-goose chase, but to Kit it was his first big
responsibility. With one of the Mexican soldiers for

a guide, he and his few men set off for the Indian village. Scouting ahead near evening, Kit found the village to be well guarded and larger than he had expected. He studied the canyon carefully, hunting for spots where riflemen could be hidden—out of range of arrows, but able to shoot into the camp.

During the night Kit placed his riflemen in these spots without arousing the guards. At daybreak he demanded the surrender of the runaways. In answer, scores of Indians poured out of the lodges. They yelled insults at their unseen enemies and shot hundreds of arrows into the surrounding brush. Again and again the howling warriors charged from the village, but the concealed trappers drove them back with accurate fire. None of Kit's men was injured, but several of the Indians were killed. Late in the afternoon they broke for the high mountains, leaving the runaways to be taken back to the mission.

Later that summer a large band of marauding Indians sneaked into the trappers' camp at night, stole sixty horses, and drove them away into the high Sierras. Again Captain Young picked Kit, gave him a few men, and sent him to bring the horses back. Kit trailed the thieves for nearly a hundred miles, surprised them at dawn over a feast of roasted horse meat, panicked the camp, killed several Indians, and brought back all but six horses which the Indians had eaten. During the rest of the expedition, Kit was recognized as the Captain's right-hand man.

With full packs, Captain Young began his return trip in the early fall of 1830. Trapping as he went, he followed the Gila River east from the great California desert. Beaver were plentiful and, when the head-waters of the river were reached in April of 1831, the packs were enormous. Captain Young was worried. He was nearing the Mexican settlements on the Rio Grande. No such quantity of furs could be brought into Santa Fe without the Mexican government's knowledge. Because he had no permit to trap in Mexican territory, the furs would certainly be confiscated. He would probably be thrown into prison.

Kit found the solution. The country was becoming familiar to him. He had hunted over it while he had been working at the copper mines. The mines were only forty miles to the east—halfway between the Rio Grande and the headwaters of the Gila. The fur packs could be hidden and covered with ore in a deep tunnel of one of the abandoned mines. Captain Young could then go to Santa Fe empty-handed, buy a permit from the governor, and return for the furs.

Captain Young sent his trappers to Taos by a roundabout route and hid the winter's catch of furs in the mines. Then he and Kit rode on to Santa Fe alone. For a sufficient bribe to the governor, permission to trap in Mexican territory could be bought. But Captain Young was not interested in such a permit. Even though the furs were well hidden, it would be dangerous to leave them long in the mines. With only a trapping permit, there would be no excuse for bringing them in to Santa Fe before the end of the next trapping season. Captain Young went to see the governor and bought a permit to trade with the Indians along the Gila River. Then he and Kit went back to the mines for the fur packs. They were sold openly in the plaza at Santa Fe for $24,000. Government officials were amazed that the Captain had been able to do so much trading with the Indians in so short a time.

Kit's share gave him more money than he had ever hoped to have. He bought himself a new Hawkins rifle, which was the best flintlock made in the United States, a fine mule, a beautiful Spanish saddle and bridle, and the best buckskin clothes in Santa Fe. When he rode into Taos, his saddlebags were heavy with Spanish silver dollars.

Money meant nothing to Kit. What he wanted was to be recognized as a real mountain man, to do the things they did, and to be one of them. Every man who had been to California with Captain Young was wealthy. They caroused, gambled, bought Taos lightning by the barrel, danced with the Mexican señoritas and loaded them with the showy, gaudy luxuries of the settlement. Within a week Kit and all the rest of them were stone broke. By fall all he had was debts, his skinning knife and his rifle.

4

Mountain Man at Last

By 1830 there were about six hundred American fur trappers in the Rocky Mountains. General Ashley had retired from the fur trade, and his interests were formed into the Rocky Mountain Fur Company. Among its leaders were Jim Bridger and Thomas Fitzpatrick, two of the most famous and daring of the mountain men. Although by the Louisiana Purchase the United States had bought only the land lying east of the Continental Divide, these men recognized no boundaries. Fearlessly they led their bands wherever mountain streams flowed and beavers built their lodges.

In the early fall of 1831, Fitzpatrick came to Taos
to recruit mountain men for the winter's trapping. The
town was full of penniless trappers, and they were all
eager to go with Fitzpatrick. He was known among
them as "Old Broken Hand" because an exploding
rifle had crippled his left hand.

As always when trapping parties were being made
up, Ewing Young's trading post was crowded. Broken
Hand stood with Captain Young behind the bar and
shouted, "This here's a skin trappin'. Them as goes,
goes for a year, traps out their gear first, and gits a
half of the over. Them as don't like it; there's the door
ye come in."

The share was not good. Broken Hand would be
getting the long end of the deal. But he was known to
be a lucky "booshway" (from *bourgeois* meaning
"property owner" or "boss"), and the Taos men were
broke. Not one of them left. Instead, they crowded
forward, shouting to be chosen. Fitzpatrick knew a
good many of the Taos men. As he looked the crowd
over, he called out the names, one after another.

As each man's name was called, he shouldered his
way up to the bar. The list of his equipment was made
out, and he made his mark in the book where Broken
Hand wrote his name. When Basil Lajeunesse's name
was called, he pushed Kit forward with him. Fitzpatrick stared sharply at the blue-eyed, bow-legged,
but solidly built boy, whose head barely reached to the

big Frenchman's shoulder. Then he looked out over the crowd again. Captain Young nudged him. In a hoarse whisper he said, "Don't ye be too hasty, Tom! That young'un makes 'em come! He ain't a-scared of nothin', and, by thunder, ye can trust his word."

Tom Fitzpatrick still looked out over the crowded room. But after Basil had made his mark, Fitzpatrick pushed the book toward Kit, glowered, and said, "Understand me right! I'll drop ye whenst and where I like; ye'll sign on for a full year if I want to keep ye, and I'll charge ye a hundred plews for your gear."

Kit made his mark, and behind it Ewing Young wrote, "Kit Carson."

Broken Hand had driven a hard bargain. "Plew" was trapper slang for a prime beaver pelt—taken from the French word *plus*. A hundred plews were worth six hundred dollars. That was a lot to be charged for a mule and saddle, half a dozen traps and a blanket. But it would have been all right with Kit if it had been a million plews. The trip to California with Captain Young had been fine, but it hadn't been into the high mountains. Kit's eyes sparkled as he headed for the corral to pick out his mule. Wagh! Mountain man at last!

With thirty picked men and over a hundred horses and mules, Fitzpatrick led his band north and turned into the mountains where Pueblo, Colorado, now stands. But he had no intention of trapping the front

range. Far beyond the Continental Divide lay the un-
trapped rivers of the Northwest—the best beaver
country in the world. Already John Jacob Astor's
American Fur Company, the Northwest Company, and
the Hudson's Bay Company were fighting for control
of this vast and wealthy region. The Rocky Mountain
Fur Company was not going to be squeezed out.
Rough, wild and dangerous as the Northwest might be,
Old Broken Hand believed he had now put together a
band of mountain men tough enough to lick it. He had
only one worry: that Carson young'un! He'd been a
fool to let Ewing Young talk him into taking a tender-
foot along. Relentlessly he drove his band northward.
He'd work the kinks out of these summer-soft hivernans and weed out the greenhorns before snow flew.

Kit didn't weed out. When the Sweetwater River
was reached, his muscles were as hard as tempered
steel and his nerves as firm as stone. October had
come, the nights were sharp, the water of the mountain streams was icy, and the fur was growing thick
on the beaver. Camp was pitched, and the men were
divided into pairs for trapping. Basil Lajeunesse
tapped Kit on the shoulder, and again they were
partners.

Unless the danger of Indian attack was great, the
Rocky Mountain trappers usually worked in pairs. A
central camp was established on the main stream,

where there was good grass for the animals. A few camp-keepers stayed with the stock, packs and provisions. The separate pairs spread afoot to the creeks and brooks that reached far back into the gorges and canyons of the snow-capped ranges. There in small basins or where the water was not too swift, the beavers built their dams and lodges.

The traps and their chains had to be heavy enough to hold a forty-pound fighting beaver. Six traps were a load for a man. Except for his blanket, rifle, hatchet and skinning knife, Kit could carry only powder horn, lead shot and a pouch for his pipe and tobacco. Near the mouth of a mountain stream, he and Basil would cut fir boughs and make themselves a wickiup—a hut not more than four feet high, open to the fire at one end, and just large enough to protect them from the night winds and snow. From this base they would separate. Each would take a side of the stream and work its tributaries to their source at the foot of the snow-caps.

Under Basil's teaching, Kit became a painstaking and expert trapper. Before entering a canyon, he would study the running water carefully for beaver sign, such as a piece of torn aspen bark or a chip gnawed by sharp teeth. When sign was fresh, he took to the stream, wading in the icy water—sometimes up to his hips—so that his scent would be carried away in the flow. Nearing a dam, he would move cautiously, watching for tracks where beaver had left the stream to cut down trees, or for a slide on the bank where they played.

Approaching a slide from midstream, he would set a trap in shallow water, with its open jaws barely covered by the soft mud of the bottom. It was placed where a beaver leaving the water to play would be apt to step on it. With such a set, a fire-hardened stake of peeled hardwood was driven into the stream bottom nearer its center. A short down-pointing fork would be left near the lower end of the stake, and the ring on the trap chain slipped over the top. A caught beaver would dive for deep water. The ring would slide down the stake, catch below the fork, and drown the beaver before he could gnaw off either the hard stake or his own leg. In deeper water the beaver followed roadways along the stream bottom. To set a trap in one of these roadways, a trapper often had to work with only his head above the freezing surface of the water.

Beaver trapping was not a job for the timid. Rising from the water dripping and half frozen, the mountain man could not wade to the bank, build a fire and warm himself. The beaver would scent him if he touched the bank within a quarter of a mile, and would be "up to trap." Then no beaver could be taken from that

A man had to wade in icy water to set beaver traps.

colony for the rest of the season. Many a trapper froze
before he could wade back downstream and get a fire
going. Alone in a wild mountain canyon, he might meet
sudden death at any bend of the stream—an Indian
arrow shot from ambush, an avalanche, a rock slide
or a mountain lion. Caught in a swift current, a man
could be tossed like a chip and drowned in a foot of
water. By a careless step on a loose stone, a trapper
might break a leg and freeze to death before his partner found him.

As the tributaries of the Sweetwater were trapped,
Broken Hand pushed his band on toward the northwest. They crossed the Continental Divide at South
Pass—in what is now southwestern Wyoming—
trapped the Green River which flows into the Colorado
and on to the Gulf of California. Then they moved to
the Bear, which flows into Great Salt Lake, and packed
over a divide to the Snake River, which twists
through the mountains for nearly eight hundred miles
before it reaches the Columbia. When, in mid-December, the beaver lodges were frozen as hard as flint, the
party was in Oregon Territory, far west of the Continental Divide. There, on the Salmon River, they went
into winter quarters.

Kit and Basil Lajeunesse had the largest fur packs
of any of Broken Hand's men. After paying Fitzpatrick the hundred plews for his outfit, Kit had two

hundred prime beaver pelts, besides marten, mink and otter, in his pack. Since leaving Taos, the band of trappers had traveled more than a thousand miles through rugged country which Kit had never seen before. Always remembering the lessons Old Kincade had taught him, he had marked every mountain, stream and canyon in his mind. Kit could have been dropped anywhere on the route they had followed and have known exactly what lay beyond in either direction.

Winter camp was the mid-season vacation of the trappers. Deer and elk skins were dressed into rawhide and stretched over poles to make teepees. With a small fire in the center, and fur packs stacked around the edges to keep out drafts, a teepee would keep six or eight men warm and comfortable through the coldest winter. Eating, sleeping, playing monte with horsehide cards, and telling stories, the mountain men enjoyed themselves until the ice should leave the beaver streams in mid-April.

Tall tales were told by the mountain men. Always the teller was the hero, and the taller the tale the better the story. "Wagh!" an old-timer would bark and roll up on one elbow. "Ever tell ye 'bout the time Alum Creek saved my life? Clostest call ever I had! I was tryin' to set trap up there in the fall of '22. Danged alum water so puckerin' my fingers shrunk halfways back into the palm of my hands. Straight-

ened up from a trap, and there was the all-firedest big
grizzly ever I seen. Wa'n't more'n six rods away, jaws
wide open, and a-comin' for me like a tornado."

Then he'd lie back and wait for someone to ask
what he did. "Do!" he'd shout. "What ye think I
done? Scooped up a hatful o' water and sot out, a-
runnin' and a-sprinklin' the trail afore my feet.
Danged alum water puckered the trail up so short I
was a-coverin' a quarter mile to a step. Sun so hot
it dried the ground afore ye could say scat, and the
trail stretched right out ag'in behind me. Wa'n't ten
seconds afore I was out ten mile ahead o' that there
grizzly."

Winter camp was the testing ground for the green-
horn. Living almost in each other's laps for four
months, no man could hide a flaw in his character or
in his courage. When spring came, Kit had passed the
test. Now he was a hivernan—a seasoned mountain
man who had wintered in the Rockies. There was no
question about Fitzpatrick's keeping him on. "That
young'un shines with me," he told Jim Bridger in the
spring. "Ye can lay store on his word, his guts and his
jedgment."

With the going out of the ice, the Fitzpatrick party
trapped back along the Snake, then the Bear, and the
headwaters of the Green. There, at Henry's Fork—
where Colorado, Wyoming and Utah now meet—they
went into summer rendezvous.

Until 1825 the trapping expeditions had been obliged to make long trips to Santa Fe, Franklin or St. Louis to dispose of their furs and buy supplies. That year General Ashley had packed supplies into the mountains. He had not established a trading post, but picked a green valley where trappers might gather, find pasture for their animals, and sell their furs or trade them for goods from the East. Though not always in the same valley, all the following rendezvous were held near the junction of the Colorado and the Green rivers.

Rendezvous was the big event in the mountain man's year. Traders from the settlements brought pack trains of goods to it. From far and near the trappers headed for the rendezvous as soon as warm weather came and the beavers started to shed their winter coats. Many of the mountain men were married to Indian squaws, and rendezvous was the time for the squaws' relatives to come visiting. Separated a short distance from the trapper's camp, hundreds of wigwams of the various mountain tribes would form villages. As many as two thousand horses, mules and Indian ponies would often be grazing in the same valley.

Money meant nothing to the mountain man. Few hivernans ever wanted to see the settlements again. The mountains had claimed them, and there they would stay till they "went under" and the wolves gnawed their bones. Rendezvous was their time to "howl," and the settlement traders were anxious to help them. At first the traders who brought goods to the mountains were reasonably honest, but this didn't last long. Mountain men and Indians were too eager for rot-gut whiskey. They would trade away anything they had to get it. By the summer of 1832 whiskey made up three-quarters of all the trade goods brought to the rendezvous. The price for a pint was a beaver plew or an Indian buffalo robe. Coffee and gunpowder were a plew or a robe a pound, blankets fifteen plews apiece, tobacco a plew a twist, and sugar a dollar a cupful.

Horse racing, shooting matches, wrestling bouts, fights, and foot races were run off—and the wagers outran the racers. Monte and poker games were going on at every fire, stakes and tempers ran high, and whiskey flowed by the gallon. At the turn of a card, a man might lose his take from a whole season's trapping. Or, from the thrust of a knife in a fight, he might be crippled for life. But there was no grieving. When a man was beat, he was beat.

Before fall the traders had all the furs and robes, and the trappers and Indians had drunk all the whiskey. With nothing left but his gun and a few rusty traps, the hivernan would head back into the mountains. The Indians would go to hunt more buffalo on the plains. At the summer rendezvous of 1832, Kit played as hard and drank as hard as the rest of the mountain men. Except for his equipment he was as broke when October came as he had been the fall before.

5

Little Chief of the Cheyennes

Leadership is a quality that is born in a man. It is usually recognized instinctively by others long before the man himself realizes he has it. Kit Carson was one of these men. Though he was only twenty-two years old, was the smallest man at rendezvous, and had not yet been in the mountains a year, he had a few staunch followers by the fall of 1832. From the time he left Franklin, he showed an unusual ability to make friends. He did not make them recklessly, but those he made remained loyal to him and looked to him for leadership all the days of their lives.

Fitzpatrick's demand of half the furs trapped by his men was too high, and Kit's contract with him had been fulfilled. At rendezvous he heard that Captain Gaunt of Taos was trapping in the valleys between the front and central ranges of the Rockies—in what is now Colorado. Gaunt was looking for top-hand trappers. He was demanding only a quarter of the catch. With his few followers, Kit crossed the mountains in three weeks, found Gaunt, and signed on with him for a year's beaver trapping.

Captain Gaunt was not a good leader. He was constantly making trouble with the Indians and was very much disliked by his own men. By mid-December they had trapped all the streams as far north as the Laramie, and south again until they were on the headwaters of the South Platte behind Pike's Peak. Gaunt took the fur packs to Taos and left his men camped on the Arkansas River.

Kit had no intention of sitting idly in Gaunt's camp all winter. He had heard that his first caravan leader, Charles Bent, was enlarging his trading post seventy miles down the Arkansas. Maybe Captain Bent would remember him and give him a job for the rest of the winter. Kit and the men who had joined Gaunt with him tossed their blanket rolls over their shoulders and headed down the Arkansas.

Charles Bent remembered Kit well and was glad to see him. The trading post was prospering. Unlike

many of the early traders, Bent and St. Vrain were
dealing fairly with the Indians. Yellow Wolf, chief of
the Cheyennes, was their good friend. Each year more
and more of the plains Indians came to the post to
trade their buffalo robes and furs for the white man's
calico and blankets. There Kit met William Bent,
Charles's younger brother, who was about his own age.
Each recognized a natural leadership in the other, and
a strong and lasting friendship grew between them.

Bent's trading post was on the north side of the
Arkansas River in American territory. But the United
States had no soldiers in the West to protect it, and a
trading post on the prairies was always liable to Indian
attack. The thriving post was to be greatly enlarged
and fortified. Logs were needed, and the nearest timber
was six miles down the river. Kit was given half a
dozen men to add to his own crew of four and was
sent to cut logs for the new fort.

The work went well. The only nearby Indians were
Cheyennes, and they were all friendly. One dark night
in February, two of them—Black Whiteman and Little
Turtle—dropped by to spend the night with the log
cutters. They picketed their ponies close to Kit's lodge.
In the morning, the two Indian ponies were the only
animals in camp. During the night a band of sixty
Crow Indians, who were raiding for horses south from
their homeland, had passed up the river. Finding the
loggers' horses and mules unguarded, they had stolen

and driven them away rapidly toward the mountains.

Kit was in a spot. Sign showed that the horses and mules had been stolen soon after dark. The Crows must have at least a twenty-mile start. Winter was howling across the prairies, and Kit and his men were afoot. He knew that the wisest thing to do would be to go to the trading post, tell Captain Bent what had happened, and let him send a strong force of mounted men to get his animals back. But Kit was ashamed to tell the Captain that he had been so careless as to leave the animals unguarded.

In California, with ten men to help him, he had recaptured Ewing Young's horses from sixty Indians. He didn't need any help against these Crows. Seeing that each man had his powder horn filled and a few pounds of dried buffalo meat rolled in his blanket, he led his little band west along the clearly marked trail left by the thieves. Black Whiteman and Little Turtle rode along, laughing at this foolish white boy who, they thought, would have to turn back.

Kit didn't turn back. For two days he dogged the trail of the Crows across the prairies and into the foothills of the Rockies. At dusk on the second day he sighted wisps of smoke rising from a grove of trees far ahead. By then his men were dead tired and had been without food for the whole day. Kit stopped his party and laid his plans for attack. The two Cheyennes were to ride ahead, circle the grove, and stand ready on the far side. Kit and his men would sneak in close to the camp. Then, as he had done with the horse thieves in California, he would make a sudden rush attack. In the confusion which was bound to follow, the Cheyennes would ride into the grove and run the horses and mules away.

The attack didn't work out as Kit had planned. When he and his men had barely reached the edge of the grove, a dog barked and came running toward them. There was a war whoop from the Indian camp, and sixty shrieking Crows came charging through the woods with drawn bows and scalping knives. There was nothing for Kit and his men to do except retreat into the open and take cover behind any bush or hummock they could find. "Hold fire!" Kit shouted to his men as he ducked behind a boulder. Waiting until the leading Indians were only a few jumps away, he barked, "Fire!"

At the roar of eleven flintlocks, the Indians turned and dashed back into the grove. Loading as they ran, Kit and his men charged in after them. The Crows raced for the clearing in the grove where they had corralled their own ponies along with the stolen animals, intending to mount and run the white men down. But the clearing was empty. Black Whiteman and Little Turtle had driven all the animals out of the grove and down toward the prairies.

Finding the grove empty, the Crows believed they

were being attacked by a strong force of white men; and, being afoot, they lost their courage. Racing on through the grove, they scattered in all directions over the prairie. Kit and his men shot after them in the gathering darkness, but there was no use in trying to follow and punish them. The camp was destroyed, and Black Whiteman and Little Turtle were found near by with the animals.

That night Kit's men were happy and proud of the boy who had led them so successfully against so large an enemy. But Kit was neither happy nor proud. As his men slept by the campfire, he lay awake and thought of the mistakes he had made. In the first place, he had been a coward not to go to Captain Bent and admit his carelessness, instead of unnecessarily risking the lives of men who trusted his judgment. In the second place, his attack had not been well planned. He had seen dog tracks on the trail and had not taken care to approach the grove from the down-wind side. But the biggest mistake of all was that he had ordered all his men to fire at once. If the Indians had not run when they did, they would have caught his whole party with empty rifles. Every one of Kit's men would have been killed before he had time to reload his flintlock. Kit would not make these mistakes again. He had also learned that no two Indian attacks could be made in the same way, and it was foolhardy to start one until every detail had been considered.

Black Whiteman and Little Turtle went back to the grove next morning to gather Crow scalps. They were surprised to find only two of the Crows had been killed in the rifle volley but they took the story of Kit's victory back to their village. A month later Chief Yellow Wolf came into Bent's trading post when Kit was there. To Kit's embarrassment, the chief made fun of the fact that with rifles against bows, arrows and knives, the white men had been able to kill only two Crows. Kit sat without letting his face show the least expression.

The old chief was wise, and he knew the sort of courage it had taken to lead so few men against so large an enemy. After he'd had his fun, he raised his arm above Kit's head in the ceremony used when a new Cheyenne chief was ordained, and his deep voice rolled through the crowded room: "My son, from this day your name among my people shall be *Vih'hui-nis*, Little Chief."

In the thirty-five years that followed, that name and the man who bore it were to be more respected, loved and feared by plains Indians of America than any other man or name in history.

6

His "Worst Difficult Experience"

When spring came, neither Kit nor his men had any wish to return and trap with Captain Gaunt. The men wanted to push into the mountains, find Fitzpatrick or Jim Bridger, and trap out the spring season with them. But Kit wouldn't go. He told them they could do as they wished, but he had signed on to trap beaver with Gaunt for a year. Much as Kit disliked Gaunt, he would not go back on his agreement. The men followed Kit, but the spring trapping expedition was a failure. The Indians dogged Gaunt's trail, killing or stealing his animals and robbing his traps.

Kit had to fight these Indians to save his own life, the lives of his followers, and the furs in their packs. By May he had driven two more brass tacks into the stock of his rifle, and his reputation as an Indian fighter began to spread through the mountains. One morning he and two of his men caught three Indians trying to steal horses in broad daylight. With a shout Kit and his men were after them. They were almost within rifle range when the Indians turned their racing ponies into a narrow gulch. Kit and his men raced after them. Fifty warriors leaped from behind boulders and bush clumps, and fifty arrows whistled around the trappers' heads. Ambush! There was no chance to turn and retreat down the narrow gulch.

The quick-wittedness that would save Kit's life a thousand times came to his rescue. "Light out!" he shouted and cut the line-ends down across his horse's rump. Straight through the center of the warriors they raced, so close that Kit's knee almost struck one brave on the shoulder. The charge was unexpected. Before the Indians could fit fresh arrows to their bow strings, Kit and his men were racing, unhurt, out of the head of the gulch. That day Kit learned another lesson about Indians which he would never forget—if Indians ran too easily, there was apt to be an ambush ahead.

Gaunt went broke during the summer rendezvous and left his men unpaid for their whole season's trap-
ʹg. With Kit's growing reputation, he might have

joined any expedition going out from the Green River rendezvous that fall, but he didn't want to. He was twenty-three now, and he wanted his own trapping outfit. With the four who were already calling themselves the "Kit Carson Men," he struck off into the high mountains of what is now southwestern Colorado and eastern Utah.

This was rough country even for mountain men. Here the Colorado River falls more than a mile as it races, white and foaming, through rock-walled canyons thousands of feet deep. Along its tributaries—the Williams, Sawatch, Blue, Eagle, Roaring Fork, Frying Pan and Gunnison—the beaver were untouched. Without compass or map, Kit and his four men fought their way through the unknown wilderness of peaks and gorges. Guided only by the mountain man's instinct, they struck eastward with the freeze-up of the beaver ponds, into the San Juan Mountains and out of them into Taos.

Their fur packs were heavy. As the little party made its way through the San Juans, Kit decided that his frivolous days were over. No more wild rendezvous and winter fandangos for him. He was going to hang onto his money, outfit big expeditions of his own, and become one of the trapper kings like Fitzpatrick and Bridger. But his resolution didn't last long. He found Taos full of mountain men on their mid-winter spree, throwing money around like sawdust, drinking Taos lightning, and stealing the Mexican señoritas away from their lovers at the fandangos. Wagh! Whoopee! They'd show the Mexican *pelados* what it took to shine with the señoritas. What was the matter with "Keet"? Was he afraid so little a man couldn't shine with the señoritas?

They had hit Kit in a tender spot. He'd show 'em what a little man could do. He did. And at the end of a week he was dead broke.

Kit had no intention of putting in a starving winter at Taos or of running into debt before the spring trapping season opened. Captain Lee, a partner of Bent's, was in town with a mule caravan of trade goods. He was anxious to reach Robidoux's Trading Post before Christmas. Robidoux's was in what is now northeastern Utah, four hundred miles across the backbone of the snowbound Rockies. Old-timers said the trip couldn't be made before spring, but Kit knew better. He had just come back from trapping the country that lay between. He hired himself and his men out to Captain Lee, led him around the southern end of the high Rockies, then up the tributaries of the Colorado River on their western side.

The day before Lee's party reached the trading post, a California Indian had stolen several of Robidoux's best horses and driven them away to the west. The trail was cold, the country extremely rough, and the Indian was known to be a crack rifle shot. Robidoux was offering a big reward for the return of his horses, and Kit needed the money. With a Utah Indian guide who knew the country to the west, he set off on the cold trail. After a hundred miles, the Utah's horse gave out, and Kit rode on alone. Not far from Great Salt Lake, he caught up with the thief in a mountain pass. There was a short, sharp fight. Kit drove another tack into the stock of his rifle and took the stolen horses back to Robidoux.

In March of 1834, Kit went with Lee to take trade goods to Fitzpatrick and Bridger, who were trapping on the Little Snake River. After the trading was done, Kit joined Fitzpatrick. But there were too many trappers in the central Rockies, and the catch was poor. After a month Kit took his few men and went to trap farther north, but they were constantly harassed by Indians.

In the Medicine Bow Mountains that spring, Kit had what he always called his "worst difficult experience." With the Indians constantly on the warpath, he had to keep his little band hidden in the mountains. It was too weak a band to go onto the plains to hunt buffalo for food, and game in the mountains was very scarce. The men had lived on the bitter meat of the beaver until they could hardly swallow it.

One day Kit found fresh sign of elk. A herd of them must be near by, probably in a high green valley. As soon as the evening camp was made, he shouldered his flintlock and struck off into the mountains afoot. There he had little fear of Indians and gave his whole attention to watching for elk sign.

Topping a brush-covered ridge, Kit discovered a little green meadow in a pocket of the hills. A grove of young quaking aspens reached into the meadow. Beyond them, half a dozen fat elk were grazing. Here was fresh meat for supper, and little more than a mile from camp; but mountain elk were as furtive as antelope. If they caught the scent of man, or if one stone were set rolling, they'd be off into the brush like scared rabbits. Kit moved cautiously, circling down wind, keeping well hidden, and working his way toward the shelter of the aspen grove. Getting within range of a fat young elk, he raised his flintlock and took careful aim.

At the report of Kit's rifle, it sounded as if an avalanche had broken loose on the hillside above him. Whirling around, he saw two enormous grizzly bears rushing at him through the brush. For a short distance, a grizzly can run faster than a race horse. Kit's flintlock was empty, and there was no chance of reloading before the bears would tear him to pieces. Dropping it, Kit streaked for the stoutest looking tree in the aspen grove. He reached it two jumps ahead of the biggest grizzly, leaped to grab a branch, and swung himself up. The ripping claw of the bear grazed his moccasin in mid-air.

Grizzly bears are the strongest animals on the North American continent and become furious when they are aroused. The male of the pair that treed Kit was aroused—and the tree was far from sturdy. It was less than six inches through at its base, and its upper branches were too weak to support a man's weight more than ten or twelve feet above the ground.

The bear, which weighed nearly a thousand pounds and was more than six feet tall, fumed and raged at the man who had escaped him. Reaching far above his head, he raked at Kit's drawn-up legs with his three-inch claws. Frothing at the mouth, he backed away and threw his tremendous weight at the slender tree. At each charge, the aspen whipped back and forth like a willow in a gale. And Kit, doubled up like a frightened raccoon, clung to it with every ounce of his strength.

Finding he couldn't break the tree down, the grizzly seemed to go insane. Raging and storming, he tore up smaller trees by their roots. Time and again he tore at the roots of the tree Kit was in, but they held.

It was well past dark before the bears left Kit and went off to feed on the elk he had shot. Waiting for the moon to rise, he watched for his chance, dropped to the ground, snatched up his rifle, and ran for camp. Boiled beaver tasted better than it had before, and Kit didn't go back to try for another elk in that valley.

By the summer of 1834, four great fur companies were fighting each other tooth and nail for the best

trappers and for control of the best beaver streams.
All the well-known streams were being over-trapped.
Daily the Indians were becoming more dangerous and
more angry at the white men who were plundering
their hunting grounds. Traders, greedy for furs and
buffalo robes, were supplying the Indians with rifles,
powder and lead. Leaders of the big fur companies
were marrying daughters of the tribal chiefs, arming
the tribes of their fathers-in-law, and setting them
against the trappers of rival fur companies.

In the northern Rockies the system had backfired.
Expedition leaders of the Hudson's Bay Company had
married among the Blackfeet, armed them with excellent rifles, and set them against the American trappers.
But the Blackfeet were an independent people. Nobler,
more intelligent, and prouder than most other Indians,
they were a nation of warriors. Whiskey would not
buy their furs and rifles would not buy their hunting
grounds—the area that is now northern Wyoming,
Montana, and southern Canada. Their streams
abounded with beaver, which they intended to keep for
themselves. To them every white man was an enemy to
be killed and robbed on sight. None but the bravest
mountain men dared venture into Blackfoot territory.

At the summer rendezvous of 1834, Kit found Jim
Bridger looking for him. Old Gabe, as Bridger was
called, was going into the Blackfoot country, and would
take none but the best mountain men with him—fifty

of them. "By thunder," he bragged, "Old Gabe's a-goin' to show them Injun varmints who this here country belongs to. Ain't no ten Injuns no place as can stand up ag'in one fust-rate mountain man." Kit and his men agreed with Bridger and joined him.

Old Gabe had underestimated the Blackfeet. Though they were not such good shots as the white men, they fought like cornered wildcats to protect their beaver streams. Bridger's band was harassed from the day it entered Blackfoot territory. Five of his men were killed, the trapping was a failure, and he was forced south to make an early winter camp on the Big Snake River in what is now Idaho.

When the snow was deep in February, a band of Blackfeet sneaked into Bridger's camp on snowshoes, and stole eighteen horses. By this time, Kit's reputation for bringing back stolen horses was well known. Bridger gave him eleven men and sent him after the stolen animals. The chase lasted for fifty miles. Kit and his men caught up to the Indians in snow so deep that the horses could not travel. But the advantage was all with the Blackfeet. There were thirty of them, and on snowshoes they could keep out of range of Kit's men and yet stay between them and the stolen horses.

Seeing that he could not win a gun fight in the deep snow, Kit called for a parley. Arms were laid down, and a meeting place was chosen on the side of a wind-swept hill. At first the Blackfoot chief seemed friendly.

He smoked the peace pipe with Kit and said he would not have taken the horses if he had known they belonged to his white brothers. But he would only return the five poorest animals. Kit soon discovered that the parley was only a trick to get the mountain men away from their rifles. As soon as they were off guard, the Indians would spring on them and overpower them by numbers. Without raising his voice or taking his eyes from those of the chief, Kit said, "Git ready, boys. Make a break for your rifles whenst I drop the pipe."

The battle was at close range. Kit had a bead drawn on a Blackfoot topknot that showed above a boulder ten yards away. Just as he was ready to squeeze the trigger, he saw another Indian with a bead drawn on Manhead—a member of Kit's own little band. Swinging his aim quickly, Kit shot and killed the second Indian. At the same instant Manhead fired, and both men were left with empty rifles. With a yell the first Blackfoot leaped to his feet and covered Kit at almost point-blank range. Defenseless, Kit could only dodge from side to side, trying to throw the Indian's aim off. The bullet ripped through his shoulder, and his right arm dropped, useless.

Without stopping to ram a fresh charge home, Manhead poured powder into the muzzle of his flintlock, dropped in a ball, bumped the stock to set the charge, and fired. As the Blackfoot fell, Kit made his retreat. Blood poured from the wound, ran down his useless arm, and trickled from his fingers. Shooting and running back, the trappers reached a clump of bushes on the top of a low hill. There they held the Indians off while beaver fur was wadded into Kit's wound in an attempt to stop the bleeding.

The Blackfeet surrounded the hill and kept firing into the bushes until dark. To have shown their position by starting a fire would have been suicide for the trappers. Kit's wound would not stop bleeding, he was weak from shock and loss of blood, and the night turned bitter cold. He and his men were sure he could not live till morning, that he would bleed and freeze to death. But the cold saved him. With the temperature well below zero, the blood oozing from his shoulder froze and sealed the wound. In the morning the Indians were gone.

Many of the men in Bridger's band had Indian wives, and several of them had gone along to keep their husbands' teepees. A squaw was a handy thing for a trapper to have. She would mind like a dog and do all the hard work around his camp. When he tired of her, he would trade her off or send her back to her tribe. Joe Meek's squaw was clever with the use of healing herbs. She tended Kit's wound till it was healed, while the men told him he was crazy not to have a squaw of his own. Kit said nothing, but he had his own opinion of squaws, of the men who married them, and of the way they treated them. One day he would have a wife of his own and a family, but he wanted nothing to do with any squaw.

In the spring of 1835 Bridger and his outfit trapped the Big Snake and the Green rivers. By the time they were ready to go to summer rendezvous, Kit's wound was entirely healed.

7

Kit the Giant Killer

The summer of 1835 saw one of the largest trapper rendezvous ever held in the Rockies. The beaver trade was at the height of its glory. More than two hundred trappers, two thousand Indians and a dozen traders were gathered in the Green River Valley. The Arapahos had set up a large camp a couple of miles down the river from the main rendezvous. They were the happiest of all the Indian tribes. They were friendly and peaceful and sang beautifully. Every evening they had a dance in a meadow by the river. Under tribal law of the Arapahos, no young man could talk to an unmarried girl without her father's consent, but the trappers were welcome to join in the dances.

When Kit and Jim Bridger came to the rendezvous, they found trouble brewing. Shunar, a giant French Canadian, had come early to the summer meeting grounds and had been bullying the trappers unmercifully. He was a tremendous fighter and had beaten dozens of mountain men to within an inch of their lives. No man in the camp dared stand up to him. The night before Kit arrived, Shunar had gone, half drunk, to a dance at the Arapaho village. He had knocked the young braves right and left, insulted the older men, grabbed the prettiest girl he could find, and tried to force his kisses upon her. Quick as a spark from flint, she had slapped his face, torn herself from his grasp, and outrun him through the trees along the river. The war chant rose from the Arapaho wigwams, and the young braves poured hot lead into their bullet molds.

With ten Indians in the Green River Valley for every white man, a massacre seemed to be in the making. Kit had been friendly with the Arapahos. As soon as he arrived in camp, he was hurried off to the Indian village to take gifts to the girl's father and to soothe his anger.

There was no soothing the Arapaho. His face was grim with anger, and his hands flew in the sign language. He would not soil his hands with the white man's gifts. His sons were now gathering their ponies to go on the warpath against them. No man's daughter could be safe from insult while a treacherous white man lived. Had not this giant white man grabbed Waanibe in his arms? Had he not chased her into the woods? If she had not been as quick as the lightning, where might she be now? The father rose and pointed his outstretched arm toward the wigwam entrance.

In the rendezvous camp, Shunar was on a rampage. Blaming Kit for having butted into his business, he had beaten two of the men who called themselves "Carson Men." When Kit came back to camp, Shunar was thumping his chest, bragging and daring any American to come near him.

Kit's anger had been burning before he saw his beaten men. Now he was furious. Walking straight up to Shunar, he looked him squarely in the eye. In the soft Kentucky drawl he had never outgrown, he said, "I reckon I'm the man you're a-lookin' for, Shunar. I'm an American, and I ain't a-scared of ye. You lay hand on one more woman or one more o' my men and I'll rip the guts out'n your braggin' hide."

It is seldom that a bully, regardless of difference in size, will risk a hand-to-hand fight with a man who is clearly not afraid of him. And Kit Carson was clearly not afraid. Shunar turned and hurried to his lodge, grabbed his rifle, leaped onto his horse, and roared that he was going to rub Kit out.

Ducking between the close-set teepees, Kit ran to his

own lodge. His best buffalo hunting pony was picketed at the entrance. Snatching a pistol from his "possible" sack, Kit vaulted onto the pony and raced toward the raging Frenchman. The pony was trained to throw its weight against the shoulder of a running buffalo. Without slackening pace, Kit hurled the pony against Shunar's heavier mount, throwing it off balance, and crowding the bully so close that he couldn't swing his rifle quickly. The advantage was all Kit's, but he didn't take it. Among the mountain men there was an unwritten code that in a gun fight both men should fire together. "Gunnin' for me, Shunar?" Kit asked as he crowded the bully.

Angling for a chance to gain the advantage, Shunar said, "No." But slowly he kept moving his rifle muzzle toward Kit's head. Kit watched the Frenchman's trigger finger. At its first flicker he dived sideways and fired. The explosions were so close together that they made a single sound. Shunar's bullet ripped through Kit's hair and powder burned the side of his face. Kit's shot broke Shunar's wrist, turned, and tore through his arm above the elbow. The rifle dropped from the bully's useless hand, and he begged for his life. But this, too, was in the mountain code. A gun fight between two mountain men was always to the death. Before Kit put the pistol back into his possible sack, he drove a brass tack into its grip.

News of the duel spread through the valley of the
Green River in a burst of cheering. Trappers from
every band rushed to shake Kit's hand and to offer him
drinks. But Kit was unhappy. His regret was not that
he had killed Shunar, but that he hadn't killed him
before the big French Canadian stirred up an Indian
war. "Shucks, boys," he told the men as he refused
their drinks, "it wa'n't a good shot. I should ought to
have put him under with the fust ball."

The mountain men were still pressing around Kit
when an Indian rider came racing up from the Arapaho
village. Waa-nibe's father wanted to see *Vih'hui-nis*. It
was important. The Little Chief must come at once.

The father was standing before his wigwam when
Kit rode through the long lines of chanting, dancing
Indians in the Arapaho village. Throwing the flap of
the lodge wide, the stately Indian extended his arm
with hand upraised above the entrance, the Arapaho
sign of welcoming a son to his father's household.
Standing just within the wigwam, his equally stately
daughter stood with her head slightly bowed. As Kit
entered, she raised her head; and in her beautiful face
and eyes he read her admiration and thanks.

Kit didn't sleep well that night, or for several
nights after. Always before him was the face of the
beautiful Arapaho girl, Waa-nibe. Never had he seen
such dignity and poise, mixed with such beauty and

Kit and Shunar clashed in a fight to the death.

charm. "Wa'n't never no señorita in Taos could shine
with that Injun gal. Wa'n't no white gal ever in Franklin as could hold a candle up to her."

Kit made it his business to visit Waa-nibe's father
often and to take him presents. Alone in the lodge, the
swarthy old Arapaho and Kit would sit, passing the
pipe back and forth between them, their hands speaking in the language of the plains. One evening, when
all but the Carson Men had left the valley of the
Green, Kit's hands asked the old Arapaho what they
had been aching to ask. As the moon rose above the
treetops along the river, the old man rose from his
place on the wigwam floor. Moving to the entrance, he
gave a low, throaty call and stood waiting. In a few
moments Waa-nibe entered the lodge. Without speaking or looking toward Kit, she crossed the wigwam
slowly and sat beside him. Chanting quietly the mar-
riage ritual of his tribe, her father swept the blanket
from his own back and tossed it over the shoulders of
Kit and Waa-nibe.

8

The Hand of the Almighty

No man could have loved a wife more than Kit loved Waa-nibe. She would be no squaw wife to drudge like a slave in a trappers' camp. She was a child, still in her teens, and should have the finest that the mountains could provide. Kit could afford it. His little band of Carson Men was growing, and he was becoming a prosperous expedition leader. He had saved carefully and invested in a string of good horses, mules and trapping gear. He bought Waa-nibe a beautiful wigwam of milk-white buffalo skins and the prettiest spotted pony he could find.

By far the best beaver streams were in the northern Rockies, and Kit was anxious to trap them. But with only a small band he would not risk taking Waa-nibe into that dangerous Blackfoot country. He might have left her with her people as some of the other expedition leaders did, but this he could not bear to do. Old Gabe Bridger was making up a strong party to trap the headwaters of the Missouri. He was taking fifty mountain men and twenty friendly Flathead Indians. Many of the men would have their Indian wives with them. There would be a well-guarded base camp where Waa-nibe would be safe and out of which the trappers would work in small groups. Kit arranged to join his little band with Bridger's.

Old Gabe was a proud and confident man as he led his expedition up the Green River, past the lofty Teton Range, and through what is now the Yellowstone National Park. Kit was equally proud as he rode beside Waa-nibe at the head of his little band. Behind them rode an Arapaho squaw, who would relieve Waa-nibe of any camp drudgery. Her pony dragged a travois, the long poles which carried the white wigwam and other camp equipment.

On the Gallatin River, at what is now the very northwest corner of Wyoming, it was discovered that another trapping party was somewhere close ahead. From the signs Kit believed it to be in trouble. Leaving

Waa-nibe with Bridger's outfit, he took his Carson Men and went to investigate.

The party was made up of twenty-four men led by Captain Joseph Gale. One of the men was Dick Owens, later to become a Carson Man and one of Kit's best friends. Captain Gale's party was in terrible shape. The Blackfeet had been hounding it unmercifully. Several men had been killed. Others, including Dick Owens, were badly wounded; and the outfit had been stripped of supplies and equipment. They were camped in a dry little valley, which was surrounded by hills and afforded almost no protection.

Next morning, while Kit was taking care of the wounded, his men set out in pairs to trap nearby beaver ponds. Soon there was shooting and whooping from beyond the hills, and the trappers came racing back into camp. Joe Meek and Liggit were the last ones in. They had dropped their rifles and were running for their lives. Behind them raced eighty well-mounted Blackfeet, shrieking and shooting their Nor'-west fusils.

The position seemed hopeless. The mountain men were trapped like mice in a bucket. With their excellent rifles, the Indians could hold the surrounding hills and pick the white men off one by one. The only cover in the valley was the tall dry grass and a thicket of dead brush on a hillside.

Kit was not yet twenty-six, but instinctively he took

The Indians could pick off the white men one by one.

command from Captain Gale. "Git your men into that brush along with the wounded and animals," he shouted. Then, to his own men, "Pour lead into them Injuns! Keep their ponies het up, so's they can't take aim!"

Kit knew Indian ponies, and he was beginning to know the Blackfeet. After a fast run the half-broken ponies would be wildly excited. A few well-placed shots would draw blood, and the smell of it would make them unmanageable. No Blackfoot would risk losing his pony by dismounting to take aim, and from the back of a plunging animal it was impossible. The Carson Men fired and reloaded in relays until Captain Gale had his battered party and the animals concealed in the thicket. Then they backed slowly toward it themselves.

From this cover the trappers were able to pick the Indians off like flies, as they circled and shot harmlessly into the brush. But the Blackfoot chief was smart. There was no water in or near the thicket. Thirst would drive the white men out more quickly and safely than bullets. He withdrew his warriors beyond rifle range and laid his siege.

The situation was more desperate than before. Kit's only hope was to goad the Blackfeet into attacking, and kill enough of them to convince their chief to abandon the fight, or frighten their medicine man with fear of a medicine stronger than his own. One of Kit's men spoke Blackfoot. Kit had him shout taunts at the Indians, daring them to fight, and insulting their medicine man. Risking an accurate Indian shot, Kit stepped out in front of the thicket, while his man shouted that here was *Vih'hui-nis,* the Little Chief of the Cheyennes, whose medicine was so strong he could send it to ride on the winds.

Possibly it was mention of the wind that gave the Blackfoot chief his idea. In any event, there was a stiff breeze blowing, the grass in the valley and the brush in the thicket were powder dry, and the Indians set the grass afire. Escape seemed impossible. The flames leaped high, the breeze was sweeping them straight toward the thicket, and the circling Blackfeet were waiting to shoot any man who might run from cover.

The onrushing flames were within a few yards of the dry brush of the thicket when the wind suddenly shifted. The fire was turned back on itself and died. Appalled, the chief sat his pony and watched the flames fade. Then with a shout he led his warriors racing out of the valley and away toward the high mountains.

Kit's own men were nearly as awe-struck as the Indians. They actually believed Kit had stopped the wind. They crowded around him, but he waved them away and told them, "Shucks, boys, this wa'n't no doin's o' mine. 'Twas the hand of the Almighty as reached out and saved us."

Though the Blackfeet made no more direct attacks

that fall, they hounded the Bridger expedition constantly. Never in sight, they skulked along the creeks
and the beaver ponds. One trapper was killed, others
were badly wounded, traps and mules were stolen, and
Bridger was forced to move into Flathead country, farther to the west. After a poor hunt the expedition went
into winter quarters near Hall's Fort on the Big Snake
River—close to the present site of Pocatello, Idaho.

During the winter Kit met Thomas McKay of the
Hudson's Bay Company at Fort Hall. McKay told him
that, as soon as spring came, he was going to trap the
Mary's River. He had never been there, but he had
heard that it was a beautiful river, far to the southwest, beyond the Rockies and the Great Salt Lake.
Beaver were said to be plentiful, and all the Indians
were friendly.

This sounded to Kit as if it might be a part of
California, that beautiful country he had visited with
Ewing Young, where it was summer all year long. Regardless of the strength of the party, the Blackfoot
country was too dangerous for Waa-nibe. On this
Mary's River in California, she would be safe, happy
and comfortable. Kit made a deal to join his party
with McKay's.

With the first greening of the spring grass, Kit
proudly led his Carson Men down the Snake River.
Waa-nibe rode with him on her spotted pony. And be-

hind rode the Arapaho servant, together with the Indian wives and children of the trappers. Where the Snake River bears to the northwest, they left it and turned south into what is now northeastern Nevada.

Stretching away to the west and south was a tremendous green valley, dotted with widely separated mountain ridges. Through it flowed a river of sparkling blue water. Certainly this looked to be a trapper's paradise. Kit knew it would be the Mary's River (now called the Humboldt). What he didn't know was that this was the head of the Great Basin Desert, in which, five hundred miles to the south, he and Ewing Young's party had nearly died of thirst. Nor could he know that the beautiful river would finally be swallowed in the desolate sands of the desert.

Beaver were abundant in the headwaters of the river. And, if there were any Indians, they kept out of sight. Kit worked south and west along the river. He was happy and proud of his lovely wife, his beautiful wigwam home, and one of the most skillful trapping outfits in the West. From Waa-nibe he was learning the language of her people and the legends which had been handed down through hundreds of Indian generations. He learned how Indians thought and reasoned, and of their resentment against the white man's taking the game which the Great Spirit had put on earth for his red children. The weather was mild, the animals fattened on the rich grass along the river, and Kit was growing wealthier with every beaver that the Carson Men caught.

As the party moved south, the grass along the river grew sparser. The river flowed more slowly and had a salty, brackish taste. Beaver were less plentiful, and little game could be found for the cook pots. Kit and McKay moved their outfits along more rapidly, feeding their parties on dried buffalo meat from their supply packs. This river must soon turn toward the Pacific Ocean in California. Maybe it joined the Buenaventura, the river that the old Spanish padres said ran through from the Rockies to the Pacific.

The farther they went, the more desolate the country became. There was no grass for the animals, no beaver in the sluggish river; and the water was too salty for drinking. Kit was worried. Without Waa-nibe, he might have pressed on for California, but the dried buffalo meat was nearly gone from the supply packs. There was nothing to do but turn back.

The trek back along the Mary's River was a nightmare. The starving mules and horses became hide-covered skeletons that could stagger only a few miles a day under their packs. Gear had to be abandoned, and the weakest of the animals butchered to feed the trappers' wives and crying children. If an animal lagged or strayed, it was stolen by sneaking Indians who were never seen. Manhead tracked down and caught two of these Indians. They were Diggers, the most primitive Indians on the continent. More like animals than men, they lived in burrows in the ground and ate roots, bugs and grasshoppers.

Nearing the headwaters of the Mary's, McKay led his famished party to the Northwest, but Kit continued toward Hall's Fort. To keep food in their wives' and children's mouths, the men had starved themselves until they were as thin as the animals. But they were hardy mountain men. Every one of them had been through starving times before, and they knew they were under the best leader in the Rockies. Kit brought them back to the little fort without the loss of a single life.

After a few disastrous seasons, Captain Wyeth, the builder of Hall's Fort, was about to go out of the fur business, and the fort was nearly abandoned. Kit decided to make it his temporary headquarters. The previous winter had been severe on the plains, and the buffalo had pushed far west into the mountain valleys. Kit found a large herd within a day's ride of the fort. Taking the best of his men and horses, he set out at once on a buffalo hunt. Enough meat must be butchered and dried to feed his band until it could regain its strength.

The hunt went well. Stores of dried meat were put away, the women and children recovered from the hardships of the trip, and the horses and mules were fattening. Then disaster struck. The Blackfeet had evidently followed the buffalo herds into the mountains.

At dawn one morning the night guard saw two men cross the courtyard, go to the corral, open the bars, and drive all the horses and mules toward the river. He thought nothing of it. It was the custom for two of Kit's men to water the animals the first thing in the morning. When the regular wranglers came out, they found the corral empty and Blackfoot moccasin tracks in the soft earth. The theft had been well planned, and a large band of Indians had been waiting at the river. They had mounted, and the animals had been driven rapidly toward the east. Kit was ruined. Nothing could be done until some trapping party came by on its way to summer rendezvous.

It was a month before a party of trappers came past Hall's Fort. Kit secured horses from the party and went with it to the rendezvous at the mouth of Horse Creek on the Green River. There Waa-nibe's baby was born. Kit was tremendously proud of his little daughter and named her Adaline.

A trappers' rendezvous was no place for Waa-nibe and the baby. All through the early spring—when Kit had been sure he was becoming wealthy—he had planned to quit the mountains, to take Waa-nibe to Taos, and to raise a large family. Now that hope was gone—at least for the present. It would take Kit's full share of the fur packs to replace the gear that had been abandoned on the Mary's River and to buy a few horses and mules. To make a new stake he would have to trap the dangerous Blackfoot country, and his wife and daughter could not go there. The only thing he could do was to take Waa-nibe and her baby to her father's wigwam.

9

The Carson Men

From the time Kit took Waa-nibe to her father's wigwam, he was determined to build the Carson Men into the strongest and best outfit in the mountains, and to establish a good home for himself and his family in Taos. He did not rush the building of his band, but he chose each man because of some outstanding quality which he admired. He never gouged the trappers in his band. Though he furnished them their entire outfits, he took only a tenth of their catch. This, and the reputation he was building for being a brilliant and fearless leader, made it possible for him to choose only the finest trappers and hunters for his Carson Men.

Kit liked boys and, probably remembering how hard it had been for him to get started, never turned a boy away because he was too young. Most of his men were in their late teens or early twenties when they joined. Oliver Wiggins, a boy who, like Kit, had run away and joined a wagon train, was picked up when he was fifteen. To Manhead, his faithful Delaware Indian, Kit added Tom Hill, who was in his early twenties, and Jonas, still in his teens but the match for almost any mountain man. Of all the tribes of Indians, there was none more noble than the Delawares, and Kit admired them. Excellent riflemen and uncanny trailers, they were trustworthy, loyal to the white men, truthful and brave.

Kit rated courage, honesty and determination in a man above size and roughness. And he had the rare ability to recognize quality in a man when he met it, regardless of the color of the man's skin. Sol Silver, who became one of Kit's leaders, was a Mexican brought up from babyhood in a Kiowa teepee. Bill Mitchell, once adopted by the Comanches and a brave of the tribe, was as much Indian on the inside as he was white man on the outside. And he knew the plains and mountains as only the Indians knew them. Quick-tempered, quick-shooting Ike Chamberlain, a terrific fighter with his fists, became manageable and a top leader under Kit's guidance.

Joe Meek was a Virginian whose cousin, James K. Polk, later became President of the United States. Joe was one of the best shots among the Carson Men. Fearless and tough as whang leather, he was a year younger than Kit. Of Dick Owens and Alex Godey, two other Carson Men, Frémont later wrote, "Under Napoleon, they might have been marshals." There was also Lucien Maxwell, follower, friend and admirer. Later he owned the largest ranch in the world, larger than the entire state of Delaware.

For the next two years, Kit and the Carson Men trapped the wildest and most dangerous country in North America and became the strongest armed force on the frontier. Their battles with the Blackfeet alone would furnish material for a large book, and their fame spread to every part of the Rockies.

When the tall silk hat became popular, the beaver trade was doomed. Kit was the first mountain man to see the writing on the wall. If he was to hold his Carson Men together, he must find other work than beaver trapping for them.

The future of the Carson Men was not all that worried Kit. Adaline was two years old and couldn't speak a word of English. His daughter would grow up as an Indian if Waa-nibe were left much longer with her people. There were no white women in the Rockies, and not a dozen on the western plains, but there was a good Negro mammy at Bent's Fort. She had been very fond of Kit when he had helped with the building of the fort. He knew she would take good care of his wife and daughter. As soon as he had disposed of his furs at the rendezvous of 1838, he took Waa-nibe and Adaline to Bent's Fort and placed them under the protection of his good friends Charles and William Bent.

Bent's Fort had grown tremendously, and most of the Indian tribes of the plains now came there to do their trading. Business between Mexico and the United States had increased. The Santa Fe Trail was a well-traveled road, and Bent's Fort was the main stopping place on the prairies. A hundred men were in Bent's employ. They, and the Indians who came with their families to trade, had to be fed. Buffalo meat was the chief food, and a thousand pounds was an average day's supply. Kit contracted to furnish buffalo meat for the fort and established the headquarters of the Carson Men in Taos.

The demand for robes in the East had resulted in the slaughter of great numbers of buffalo. The big herds no longer roamed near the trails and rivers but kept to the barren prairies as much as possible. It was impossible to supply Bent's Fort with fresh meat from day to day. Twice a year, as the herds migrated, they had to be followed far into the barrens, hundreds of them killed, their meat dried and packed back to the

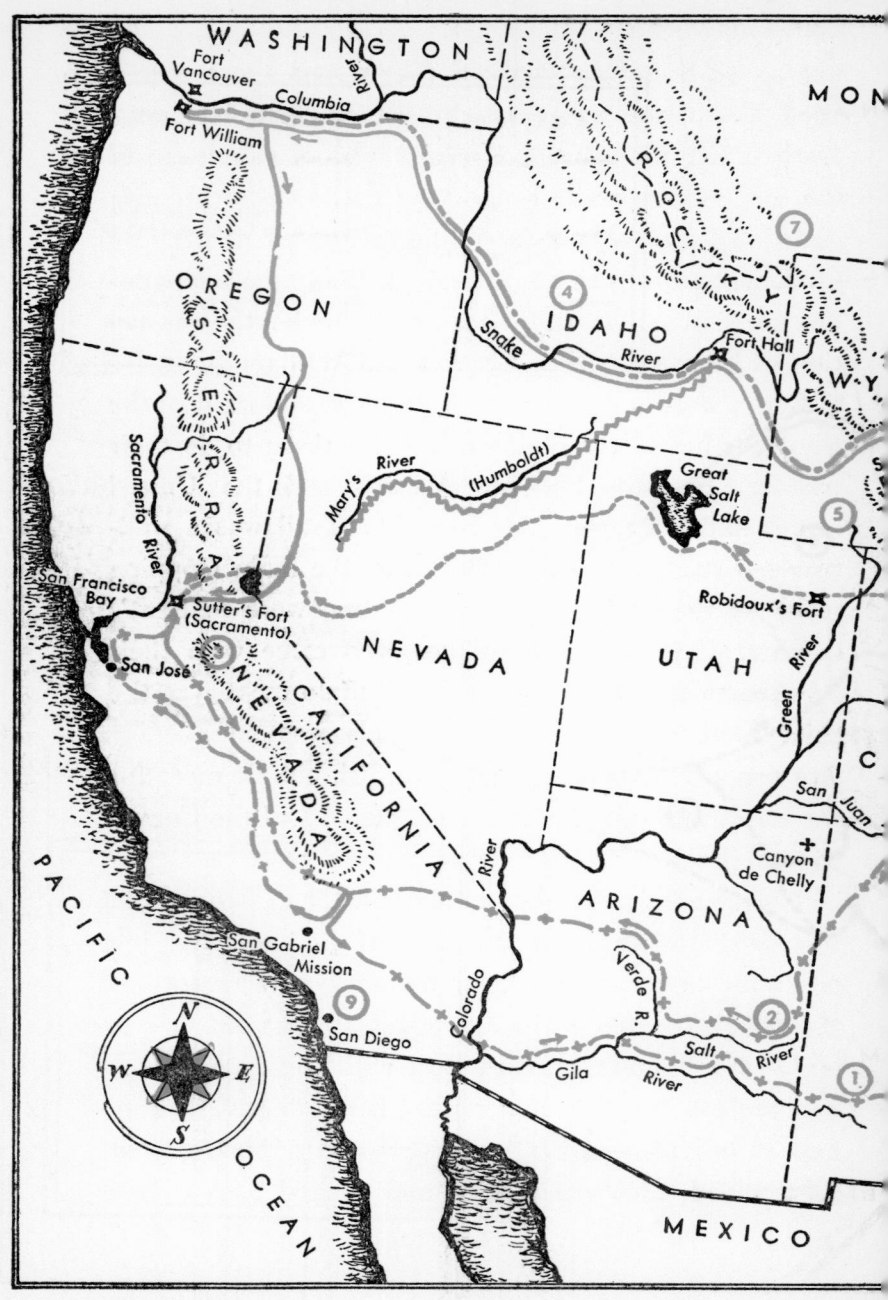

A GUIDE TO THE VARIOUS ROUTES MENTIONED IN THIS BOOK

- Santa Fe Trail
- Mary's River Expedition
- Ewing Young's California Expedition 1829-30
- Frémont's Expedition to California 1843-44
- Oregon Trail
- Route by which Kit Carson led Frémont to California — 1845

KEY TO THE LOCATION OF THE HAPPENINGS IN THIS BOOK

1 Copper Mines where Young hid the fur packs
2 First Brass Tack earned by Kit Carson
3 Young's horses recaptured by Kit Carson
4 Fitzpatrick's winter camp 1831
5 Green River rendezvous and Kit's fight with Shunar
6 Kit's "worst difficult experience"
7 Kit's battle with the Blackfoot Tribe
8 Comanche Fight 1838
9 Kearny's battle with the Californios
10 The Battle of Adobe Walls

fort. Hunting was becoming very dangerous. The plains Indians were furious at the white men for killing their buffalo. More and more often they were on the warpath against them.

During the first hunt Kit established his reputation, his name, and the strength of his medicine with the plains Indians. With Bill Mitchell, Joe Meek, and three of his Delaware Indian hunters, he had set off for the buffalo range on the dry, barren prairies to the south of the Arkansas. One morning when they were eighty miles from the nearest water, Bill Mitchell pulled his mule up suddenly and studied a knob on the low hill ahead. "Comanche!" he said as the knob disappeared. "Wearin' paint! There's aptly a right smart parcel o' braves t'other side of that rise."

Like the howl of a thousand hungry wolves, the war whoop of the Comanches seemed to come from all directions. The thunder of pounding hoofs rolled across the prairie; and two hundred naked, painted warriors came racing over the brow of the hill. The sun gleamed on the blades of their eight-foot lances as, led by their chief, they charged down upon the half dozen hunters.

At the first shriek of the Indians, Kit's pack animals had stampeded, carrying with them the water supply, extra powder, lead and food. There was no tree, bush or cover of any kind within miles. The men had only seconds to prepare for the charge. Leaping from his saddle, Kit snatched his hunting knife from its sheath.

"Kill your mule!" he shouted and slashed the blade across the throat of his rearing animal. With the mules still kicking on the ground, the men threw themselves flat behind them, yanked the stoppers from the muzzles of their flintlocks, and shook fresh powder into the firing pans. "Hold fire!" Kit shouted to Mitchell and Meek. Then to Manhead, Tom Hill and Jonas he snapped, "Git the chief!"

As the chief and his war horse fell, the racing band of Indian ponies split and swept around the dying mules. Heedless of the loss of their chief, the Comanches wheeled and charged back again, expecting to catch the hunters with empty rifles. This time the white men's rifles barked, three Comanches pitched headlong to the prairie, and the charge split again, but only for seconds. Before the Delawares could reload their rifles, the Comanches had yanked their plunging ponies back to the charge.

Except for the sureness of Kit's leadership, he and his men would have been cut to shreds and trampled under the pounding hoofs within seconds. But Kit knew plains horses and had planned well. At the smell of the warm mule blood, the Indian ponies became crazed. Bucking and rearing, the lead ponies stampeded the whole band. Before their riders could bring them under control, six flintlocks were reloaded and leveled over the dead mules. As one Comanche after another forced his plunging pony close enough for a bow shot, he was brought down by the steady aim of a hunter.

Again and again the Indians pulled away, steadied their ponies and charged. Each time, their frightened mounts veered off before they reached the carcasses. The Comanches threw their lances down, lay flat along their ponies' backs and, on each sweep past the barricades, sent a whistling storm of arrows at the hunters. And on each howling, shrieking sweep, three flintlocks barked, and three held fire.

With their ponies frothing and winded, the Comanches withdrew to the hilltop for a council. It was long. Their loss of braves had been heavy, and they could see that no hunter was badly wounded. At a signal from their new chief, the Indians rode out in single file, circling the trapped hunters just beyond the range of their flintlocks. Watching them, Kit knew their strategy as well as if he had been at their council. The Comanche was the fox of the prairie. When attack failed, he would use cunning. Thirst and heat would win where lances and arrows had failed.

The noon sun beat down, heat waves shimmered up from the barren prairie, the barrels of the rifles burned like hot coals, but still the Comanches circled. Through the afternoon the hunters' lips swelled and cracked. Kit had made his plan, but it wasn't yet time. Taunting, howling, and making signs as if drinking, the circling Comanches rode at a slow walk.

Near sunset Kit crept to Bill Mitchell's side. Bill

knew the Comanche language. He was to shout taunts at the Comanche medicine man and tell him his medicine was as antelope milk compared to the strong medicine of *Vih'hui-nis*. If it were not, the Comanches would fear bullets no more than the white men feared arrows. Was the Comanche afraid of his own weak medicine? Was that why he had no heart to fight, but skulked the prairie like a cowardly coyote, afraid of the white man's camp? If the medicine man could count, let him count the number of Comanche dead and the number of *Vih'hui-nis'* dead. When darkness came, *Vih'hui-nis* would scatter his strong medicine on the night wind, and the weeping squaws would come in the morning to gather the Comanche dead.

Kit knew the power of the tribe's superstitions. If they lost faith in their medicine man or the strength of his medicine, they would be sure it was because stronger medicine was being used against him. In battle, if his medicine failed, he must kill himself or be forever shamed. The Comanche medicine man would have no choice; he would have to gather his warriors and lead them against the one who claimed stronger medicine.

The strategy worked. Dancing, chanting, and waving charms, the medicine man worked himself and the Comanche warriors into a frenzy. Then, leaping on his pony, he raced ahead of them toward the shouting hunters. He would show them his medicine was strong enough to turn bullets. He himself would cut the heart from this bragging, bow-legged *Vih'hui-nis*.

Holding his men back, Kit stepped out a few paces to meet the charge. As the Comanches raced into rifle range, he raised his flintlock and lined his sights. Moving them slowly until the paint-streaked throat of the medicine man showed dead-center, he squeezed the trigger and dropped flat. More than a hundred arrows whistled over him. The charge split and swerved past. As Kit jumped to his feet, the medicine man's body lay twitching a dozen yards away.

The Comanches did not turn to charge again but swept on to the top of the hill. There they gathered for another council. This one was not long. Seeing Kit standing over their fallen medicine man, they evidently decided his brand of medicine was too strong to be trusted on the night wind. After a few minutes they mounted and disappeared beyond the hill.

Among all the Indian tribes the strong medicine of *Vih'hui-nis* became a legend, and it was a brave chief who led his warriors against the Carson Men. Still, Kit remained the quiet, soft-spoken, bandy-legged Kentucky backwoodsman. His only bragging was done to goad an Indian medicine man into an unwise attack, and he was shy of taking credit for his brilliant feats.

Before the last rendezvous of the fur trappers was held in 1840, the Carson Men at Taos numbered more than forty. Little of their time was spent on beaver trapping. Right from the beginning Kit had demanded the same honesty, straightforwardness and courage from his men that he demanded from himself. Trouble was avoided when possible; when impossible, it was met head on. No honest Indian feared the Carson Men, and no thief or murderer dared face them.

Settlers were moving into the fertile plains west of the Missouri River. The Santa Fe, Overland and Spanish trails were becoming well-traveled roads; and the Indian's resentment of the whites was growing by leaps and bounds. Settlements and ranches were being raided; caravans were being plundered and travelers killed. Kit had no trouble in keeping the Carson Men busy, guarding caravans on the trails, hunting game for the settlements, and recovering stolen property from the Indians.

During this time Waa-nibe lived in her milk-white wigwam just outside the gates of Bent's Fort, and Adaline grew into a beautiful child. Kit spent as much time as he could with them, but it was never enough. His work with the Carson Men kept him in the saddle most of the time. There was hardly a spot throughout the prairies and mountains that he didn't cover, but always he planned for the day when he and Waa-nibe would have a quiet home in Taos, and could settle down to raising their family.

That day was never to come. Riding out of the Rockies one spring morning, Kit met a messenger bringing him word that Waa-nibe was sick. She had the prairie fever that was sweeping through the Indian tribes. He rode a hundred and eighty miles in two days to reach Bent's Fort and got there just in time for Waa-nibe to die in his arms.

Broken-hearted, he turned back to the mountains to bear his sorrow alone by the beaver streams. But he couldn't abandon Adaline and the Carson Men. Adaline worried him. He couldn't let her grow up an ignorant child, neither Indian nor white, in a frontier trading post. He had never seen any sense in book learning for himself, but his daughter must grow up to be an educated lady. In the spring of 1842, he took her back to Missouri, to live with his sister and attend a convent in St. Louis.

10

Pathfinder for the Pathfinder

During the ten years since Kit had gone into the Rockies with Broken Hand Fitzpatrick, great changes had taken place on the North American continent. Hundreds of thousands of Europeans had migrated to America, and the country east of the Missouri River was becoming too crowded for pioneers. All the land west of the Missouri had been considered a worthless desert. The eastern Indian tribes had been driven into this desolate region. In a treaty of peace, it had been granted to them forever. But American pioneers were constantly pushing beyond the river.

By the Louisiana Purchase, the United States had bought the land as far west as the Continental Divide, but this boundary meant little. The American mountain men had never recognized any boundary as they pushed west across the mountains for beaver. The Mexicans had refused to give up any territory south of the Arkansas River; but a new, independent republic had been carved out of it. In 1835 the American settlers in Texas had revolted against the Mexican government. Sam Houston had licked the Mexicans in the Battle of San Jacinto in 1836, and had set up the Republic of Texas, independent of both the United States and Mexico.

The weak Mexican government had much more trouble than this on its hands. California was becoming famous for its wealth and climate. Both France and England coveted it and were eagerly watching for an opportunity to grab it. Both countries had made large loans to Mexico, which they considered as mortgages on California; and both were anxious to foreclose.

In the Northwest the situation was even more involved. In 1543 Bartolome Ferrelo had discovered this coast and claimed all the territory for the Spanish. In 1579 Sir Francis Drake, and in 1778 Captain James Cook, had charted the coast and claimed the land for England. In the meantime, the Russians had pushed south from Alaska and claimed it. In 1792 Robert Gray had sailed up the Columbia River, named it for his ship, and claimed all the land it drained for the United States. Lewis and Clark also had laid claim to the Northwest by virtue of their exploration in 1805. However, the Hudson's Bay Company had established trading posts and forts there. Following the War of 1812, the whole Northwest had become disputed territory, claimed jointly by England and the United States.

In Washington there was considerable difference of opinion regarding this vast territory between the Missouri and the Pacific. Many senators considered the whole region to be desolate and not worth fighting for. Others thought it foolhardy to expand the territory of the United States beyond the ability of its military power to control. They pointed out that, though the United States had purchased all the land south of the Arkansas, it had never been able to spare enough military strength to secure this territory from the Mexicans. Still others were all-out expansionists and wanted the United States to seize the whole North American continent.

Among these rabid expansionists was Senator Benton of Missouri. He was a shrewd, far-seeing politician and had great power in the United States government. He knew that the hold of Britain on the Oregon region and of Mexico on California were not strong. He did not believe that the future of the United States was secure unless it controlled the western coast of the continent. Reasoning that the final ownership of the great region west of the Rockies would fall to the country having the largest number of settlers there, he was determined to stimulate the westward movement of American emigrants.

Following the route taken by traders going to the mountain men's rendezvous, the Oregon Trail had become a well-known wagon road through the mountains. By the spring of 1842 several hundred American pioneers had moved their families over it to the rich farming lands along the Columbia River. Fear of Indians and the hardships of the trail had kept thousands of others from following. Senator Benton knew this fear must be broken down.

The Senator's newly acquired son-in-law, John Charles Frémont, was a lieutenant in the Geographic Department of the government. Why not use him to overcome this fear? Frémont was a good surveyor, a map maker and an excellent writer. The East was hungry for news of the West. If he could lead an expedition over the Oregon Trail, write his reports to read like an adventure story, and make the trip sound safe and easy, it would certainly stimulate the westward movement. On the pretext that the purpose was to map the Oregon Trail to the Continental Divide, Senator Benton pushed through a congressional appropriation for an expedition and Frémont's appointment as its leader. To make it look like a vacation trip into safe country, he sent along his twelve-year-old son and his nephew.

Kit Carson was still in St. Louis when Frémont came there to hire men and outfit his expedition. Among those he employed was Lucien Maxwell, who had been one of the Carson Men. Either by chance or by Lucien's planning, Kit started west on the same river boat which carried the Frémont expedition. Before it reached Westport Landing—now Kansas City—the two men had met. They liked each other, and Frémont engaged Kit at a hundred dollars a month to act as his guide.

Except for bravery, endurance and size, it would have been difficult to find two men more different than John Charles Frémont and Kit Carson. Frémont was of the French Creole type—sharp-featured and hawklike, with a high forehead, thick wavy brown hair and a full beard. He was highly nervous, impetuous almost to the extent of recklessness, and obstinate. At the same time he was very well educated, speaking and writing flawless French and English. Trained as a navigator, Frémont could determine his exact location and chart his course on either land or sea.

Kit was Scotch-Irish, blond, cautious, steady-nerved and determined. Unable to write his own name, he spoke the dialect English of the frontier, the Mexican peon Spanish, the Canuck French of the Canadian

mountain men, the Indian dialects of the Arapahos,
Cheyennes, and Comanches, a smattering of Blackfoot,
and the sign language of all the tribes. He knew nothing of instruments and had never owned a watch or
compass. But stored away in the back of his mind there
was a picture of every stream, canyon or mountain he
had ever seen. Frémont was twenty-nine, and Kit was
three years older.

Much as Kit liked the young Lieutenant, he had little confidence in Frémont's ability to lead an expedition into the mountains and still less confidence in the
men he had hired for his party. Most of them were
French Canadian voyageurs. And having the young
boys along worried Kit. Actually no guide was needed
to follow the Oregon Trail, but to travel it was becoming more dangerous every day. Indians, who had once
been friendly, had been driven onto the warpath by
the mistreatment, cheating and greed of the whites who
were pouring into the West.

The Sioux had sworn to drive all white men from
their hunting grounds and were known to be camped
along the Oregon Trail from the foothills to the South
Pass. That spring of 1842, several old-timers of the
mountains had been killed, wagon trains had been
plundered, and emigrants tortured. Without Frémont's
knowledge, Kit sent a messenger riding to Taos. The
Carson Men were to be waiting at Fort Laramie when
Frémont's party reached there. They were not to let

themselves be seen, but were to guard the expedition from the foothills to South Pass and back. The cost to Kit was way beyond the hundred dollars a month Frémont had agreed to pay him.

As might be expected, there was soon a clash of wills between these two strong-minded men. Kit felt it would be too dangerous to take the boys into the mountains. To prove to Easterners the safety of the Oregon Trail, Frémont was bound he would take them along. At Fort Laramie it came to a show-down, and Kit won it without an argument. He simply dictated his will to the clerk at the fort. When word of it got around, the French Canadians were frightened and ready to turn back. If the mountains were so dangerous that the famous Indian fighter had made his will, it was too dangerous for them, and certainly too dangerous for small boys. The Lieutenant was forced to compromise; the boys stayed at Fort Laramie, and the voyageurs went on.

The Carson Men, who had fanned out around the expedition as it moved, caught a couple of Sioux braves and convinced them that it wouldn't be a good idea to attack the Frémont party. Otherwise the trip to South Pass and back was uneventful. Although from this trip Frémont won the name of "The Pathfinder," he found no path that the mountain men hadn't been traveling for twenty years. At first he had been furious with Kit for making his will and nearly breaking up the expedition. But by the time they got back to Fort Laramie, each man had learned to admire and respect the qualities of the other. They parted warm friends, and Kit promised to guide Frémont again if his services should ever be needed.

From Fort Laramie Kit led his men back into the mountains for the fall beaver trapping. But with the freezing of the streams, he did not go into winter camp. There was something in Taos that he wanted more than all the beaver pelts in the world. Ever since he had first gone into the mountains, he had wanted a home and a family of his own. His friend, Charles Bent, had married the daughter of Don Francisco Jaramillo, one of the leading citizens of New Mexico. Before taking Adaline back to Missouri, Kit had visited his friend's home and had met Bent's sister-in-law, Señorita Josefa.

Josefa was not quite fifteen, but Mexican girls grow up early, and Josefa was a mature and cultured woman. Tall, willowy, and highly intelligent, she had the striking brunette beauty of her Spanish ancestors. With it she had the calm dignity of her Aztec Indian forbears. From the moment Kit saw Josefa he had loved her, and she had found equal love for the quiet, self-reliant mountain man who was so different from the men of her own race. On February 6, 1843, "Cristover Carson & Maria Josefa Jaramillo" were married in the old adobe mission church in Taos.

Taos was no longer the bustling headquarters town of the trappers. With the passing of the beaver trade, it had settled back into a sleepy little Mexican village. Its one claim to fame was that it was the headquarters for the Carson Men. Kit bought Josefa a house on the plaza and thought his days of roaming were over. He would settle down now, direct his band of Carson Men from Taos, and raise a large family.

Again he was disappointed. All spring he had to keep leaving his wife to track down marauding Indians, to help avoid a battle between the Mexicans and the Texans, and to recover stolen animals. In May Frémont, who was still in the Geographic Department of the government, came west on another expedition. He had Kit's promise of the year before and again wanted him for his guide. To Kit a promise was a promise. Much as he hated to, he left Josefa in Taos and went to join Frémont.

While Kit had been busy in the West, Frémont and Benton had been equally busy in the East. Frémont had written glowing stories of the Oregon Trail, the beauties of the Rockies, and the wealth of the Columbia River Valley, which he had never seen. The Senator had seen to it that these stories were published in all the papers, and thousands upon thousands of copies were printed by the government and distributed throughout the East. Great wagon trains were being made up for the Oregon Trail, and Frémont had become a national hero. In fact, he had received so much publicity as Pathfinder, Dauntless Explorer, and Conqueror of the West, that he had incurred the jealousy and hatred of many of the Regular Army officers.

This was not helped a bit in the spring of 1843. Senator Benton had been successful in convincing Congress to appropriate another large sum of money for a new Frémont expedition. Presumably this one would map and relocate the entire Oregon Trail all the way to the Pacific, so as to make it shorter and easier for American immigrants to the Northwest. Actually Senator Benton had other fish to fry. It might be time for the American settlers in Oregon and California to do as the settlers in Texas had done: set up independent republics, which might later be annexed to the United States. It is believed that Frémont's secret mission was to stir up such revolts if it looked as though the time was ripe.

Frémont himself had not helped his position with the army officers. As a lieutenant in the Geographic Department, he had no authority to take arms into a disputed or foreign territory. However, when he made up his second exploration party in St. Louis, he chose thirty-nine experienced fighting men. He armed them to the teeth, and hoodwinked Colonel Stephen Kearny, commander of the St. Louis arsenal, into supplying him with a mounted cannon for protection against "the audacious Indian tribes." When word of this reached Washington, orders recalling Frémont were immedi-

Frémont insisted on dragging the cannon with them.

ately issued, but he was tipped off by a messenger sent post haste by his wife. He slipped away into the prairies before the order arrived.

Again Kit set his Carson Men to guarding the Frémont expedition, but this time the men did not see it through. Frémont was bound to find a central pass through the Rockies which would not only shorten the Oregon Trail, but provide a direct route from the Missouri River to California. Kit told him that no pass existed over which wagons could be taken, but the Lieutenant set out to show him he was wrong. He spent so much time examining impassable canyons in the high Rockies, and exploring the Wind River Range and Great Salt Lake, that winter caught him near Hall's Fort, where the Blackfeet had stolen Kit's horses.

Both Kit and his Carson Men thought it foolhardy to try to cross the western mountains in the dead of winter, but Frémont became obstinate. He had set out to show the world how simple and safe the Oregon Trail was, and he wasn't going to let a little thing like winter in the mountains stop him.

Kit had promised to guide Frémont, and that was that. The fact that it might cost him his life made no difference, but he wouldn't risk the lives of his Carson Men unnecessarily. He told them either to go into winter quarters or to return to Taos. With the exception of Alex Godey, the men turned back. Alex would not leave Kit so he joined Frémont's party.

The fight north and west from Hall's Fort to the Columbia River Valley was heartbreaking. In good weather the mounted cannon had been a tremendous handicap over mountain trails. In deep snow it was an anchor, but Frémont would not abandon it. He had brought it to impress the British and Mexicans, and he was going to take it through at any cost. It did cost the lives of many mules and threatened the lives of the men. Half-starved, ragged and nearly frozen, they eventually dragged it to the Dalles of the Columbia, a hundred miles up river from the British Fort Vancouver. Leaving Kit with most of the men and all the equipment, Frémont went down the Columbia by boat, bought provisions and returned. He had evidently decided not to impress the British with the cannon and that the time for revolt in Oregon was not ripe.

Winters are never severe in the valley of the Columbia, and Kit had told Frémont that the winters along the California coast were as warm as summer. Though neither he nor Kit knew what lay between, and against Kit's advice, Frémont decided to set out at once for California. He would do his impressing on the Mexicans. Hiring a couple of local Indians as guides, and abandoning all wheeled equipment except the cannon, he turned his expedition toward the south. Kit saved it from disaster.

The Indian guides led the party into the Klamath Marshes of northern California, became completely lost and deserted. Ahead and to the west lay the high snowcaps of the Sierra Nevadas. Frémont decided to turn east. Kit knew the Great Basin could not be far away in that direction, and Frémont had an old map showing the Buenaventura River cutting straight through the Sierras to the Pacific. They would move down the basin to the Buenaventura and follow its course through the mountains.

After tremendous hardships the expedition reached the Truckee River Canyon (just east of where Reno, Nevada, now stands) on January 17, 1844. The supplies were exhausted; the men became rebellious and wanted to make winter camp. Frémont was still sure the Buenaventura would be reached any day and insisted on pushing southward. When, at the end of the month, Kit discovered the Carson River flowing out of the high mountains, the condition of the expedition was serious. Horses and mules were dying rapidly for lack of food. Men were eating the animals' stringy flesh to keep from starving. The search for the Buenaventura was given up, and the cannon had to be abandoned.

Frémont took observations from the stars and discovered that it was only a hundred miles to Sutter's Fort in the Sacramento Valley, but the high Sierras lay between. A young Washoe Indian was found who took Frémont and Kit to his tiny village. There the old men told them that no man could live to cross the mountains in winter. The situation was desperate. The Indians could spare no food, it was too late to turn back, and the men and animals were too weak to go into winter quarters. A way had to be found across the Sierras.

After studying the mountains carefully, Kit picked the only route that looked possible. All packs were abandoned, and by February 4th the party had fought its way to the 6,700-foot level. Here an upland valley was found with forage for the animals. But beyond, the snow was too deep, and the temperature at noon was below zero. Kit made snowshoes for himself and Frémont, and together they searched for a pass between the high peaks. On February 6th, from the top of a saddle back 9,000 feet above sea level, they could look away to the west across the ragged mountain peaks. Suddenly Kit caught Frémont's arm and pointed toward the dim outline of Mount Diablo, just east of San Francisco Bay. "There is the little mountain," he said. "It is fifteen years since I seen it, but I'm just as sure as if it had a-been yesterday."

The job was not finished with the finding of the pass which is still known as Carson Pass. To get the men and animals over it, the snow crust had to be broken for nine miles with mallets, the snow tramped into a firm trail and lined with spruce boughs. On February 20th Kit led the party over the pass without the loss of a single man. On March 6th they reached Sutter's Fort. Only thirty-three of the one hundred and four horses and mules with which they left the Dalles were still alive. Two of the men had gone insane from hardship, frost and starvation.

Frémont was in a poor condition to impress anybody. He had found no new route through the Rockies and had not shortened the Oregon Trail by one inch. Without Kit Carson, he would have lost his own life and the lives of his men. It was not until he reached California that he discovered there was no such river as the Buenaventura.

11

Conquest of California

After re-outfitting at Sutter's Fort, Frémont started east over the Old Spanish Trail. Far out in the California desert they found a grief-stricken eleven-year-old Mexican boy. A band of more than sixty Indians had left the boy to die of thirst after killing his father and mother and stealing the herd of horses they were driving on the trail. Frémont and Kit were furious at the cruelty of the Indians.

As a United States officer in a foreign country, Frémont could not hunt down and punish the murderers, but he gave Kit permission to do so, with whatever volunteers would join him. Only one man had courage enough to volunteer for such a dangerous mission— Kit's own Carson Man, Alex Godey. Alone the two men set out on the trail of the savages, followed it a hundred miles into the mountains, surprised and stampeded the camp, killed two Indians and recovered the horses. Frémont told the story well in his report of the expedition, and Kit Carson's fame spread throughout the world.

Kit had no interest in fame. His interest was in a home and family. The old West was passing rapidly, settlers were pouring into the prairie country, buffalo were scarce along the trails, and there was a demand for beef to feed the caravans. After Frémont had returned to Washington, Kit and Dick Owens bought a ranch and set out to become New Mexico's first cattle raisers. The venture was short-lived. The buildings were barely completed and Josefa moved to the ranch when Frémont came west again. It is evident that this time he told Kit the real reason for his expedition.

The situation in California was boiling. The Mexican hold on the territory was slipping badly. The United States had offered twenty-one million dollars for California, but Mexico had refused it. Both the British and French had warships just off the coast, watching for the right moment to move in, seize control, and raise their flags. There were now six hundred American settlers within a hundred miles of San Fran-

cisco Bay. James K. Polk, the new President, was anxious to secure California for the United States.

Without it the future of the country would not be
safe. It was high time for the American settlers to be
stirred into revolt. There was not a moment to lose;
the expedition must get to California with all speed.
There was no hesitation on Kit's part; the future of
the United States was more important than anything
else. He and Dick sold out at a big loss and joined
Frémont on August 3, 1845.

There seems to have been no secrecy between Kit
and Frémont on this third expedition. Instead of trail-
ing along as guards, the Carson Men were employed as
members of the expeditionary force. Frémont now had
complete confidence in Kit's wisdom and let him choose
the quickest route to California.

Kit's knowledge of the Rockies was so complete that
he was able to lay out his route through the unmapped
mountains as accurately as a motorist now lays out the
route of his vacation trip. Rapidly he led Frémont
west, along the Arkansas River to its impassable
gorge, then turned north into the South Park behind
Pike's Peak. Modern engineers have not been able to
improve on his course from there to the Colorado
River, and automobile route 24 now follows it through
the backbone of the high Rockies.

Crossing a low divide to a tributary of the White
River, Kit led on toward the site where Robidoux's

trading post had stood. From there to the Great Salt Lake, the trail was as fresh in Kit's mind as if he had been over it the day before. It was over this route that he had trailed the California Indian who had stolen Robidoux's horses twelve years earlier. West of the lake, no direct route to California was known, but it was there that Kit thought the greatest saving of time could be made.

South and west of the great lake, a deep layer of salt covers the earth for more than sixty miles. Beyond lies the Great Basin Desert, four hundred miles wide and a thousand miles long. When Kit had trapped the Mary's River, he had correctly guessed that this was once an inland salt sea, that the water had all evaporated—except for the lake itself—and that the dozens of small ranges of mountains had once been chains of islands. If this were so, the salt would not have ruined the soil on the mountains; there would be fresh water and grass for the animals.

No man had ever crossed the salt flats, and only two —Jed Smith and the hardiest man in his band—had lived to cross the desert. Both had been temporarily crazed by thirst and sunstroke. But any direct route to California must be over the flats and the desert, and Kit believed a crossing could be made. Taking Basil Lajeunesse and Lucien Maxwell, he set off late in the afternoon for the distant mountains which showed beyond the salt flats. They traveled at night to avoid the terrific heat of the sun's reflection on the salt. If the mules should die on the way or if no water were found at the mountains, there would be no possible hope for the men.

Frémont was to watch with a telescope, and Kit was to light a huge bonfire if he succeeded in crossing the flats and finding grass and water. Just before dawn Frémont saw a tiny speck of light far to the west. The next night the expedition, with two hundred animals and sixty armed men, crossed the salt flats without the loss of a single life. Automobile routes 40 and 50 now cross the salt flats on the line of Kit's first crossing.

From this point Kit laid an almost straight course across the desert in the direction of Sutter's Fort. He was gambling that his first judgment of this desert had been right. Short mountain ridges ran north and south, separated thirty or forty miles from each other. Water, grass and game were found on most of them. With Kit and his Carson Men scouting ahead, the desert crossings between the ridges were made at night. The animals rested and grazed during the heat of the days. Still without the loss of a single man or animal, Kit led the expedition over the desert, the high Sierras, and down to Sutter's Fort in the Sacramento Valley of California on December 9th. This was two months faster than any previous crossing of the West had been made. And the speed of this expedition may have had tremendous effect upon the proper timing of the California revolt.

Many books have been written on the conquest of California, and there are few that do not give Frémont credit for the great part he played in it. It is true that he acted without official authority, and that he was often rash, high-handed and disrespectful. However, there is little doubt that he was following private instructions from Senator Benton and possibly from an even higher source.

In any event, he did stir up a revolt, raised the American flag before the British realized what was going on, coöperated fully with Commodore Stockton of the United States fleet, and fought gallantly when he could induce the Mexican generals to fight. The final surrender was made to him. During the whole campaign, Kit and his Carson Men were the backbone of Frémont's little army. In his reports he wrote, "Carson, Owens, and Godey would have been marshals under Napoleon."

Since Stockton was an officer of the armed forces of the United States and Frémont belonged to the Geographic Department, the Commodore publicly declared the whole of California to be a territory of the United States, named himself Military Commandant, and appointed Frémont Civilian Governor.

It was important to get news of the capture of California to Washington as quickly as possible. Kit was commissioned a lieutenant in "the United States Navy Battalion of Mounted Riflemen" and was given dispatches to deliver personally to President Polk within sixty days. Taking fifteen of his own Carson Men and fifty of the best horses and mules at Frémont's command, he set off on September 5, 1846. Neither men nor animals were spared in the race eastward across the Mojave Desert and up the Gila River. Sixty days was a short time in which to make a trip that had never been made in less than six months.

In the south the war with Mexico was going well for the United States, but nothing was known in Washington about the situation in California. General Stephen Kearny was placed in command of the Army of the West, and given orders to capture Santa Fe, then to move on for the conquest of California. This was the same Stephen Kearny whom Frémont had hoodwinked into furnishing him with the cannon for his second expedition. The Governor of Santa Fe had surrendered without a shot being fired, and Kearny had started on for California, leaving New Mexico with no military protection. With him he had Broken Hand Fitzpatrick as guide, two hundred mounted dragoons, and a long train of heavy wagons.

In the meantime, Kit had been driving hard up the Gila River, carrying news of the conquest of California. Though he had broken down thirty-four of his

best animals and fought several Indian skirmishes, he
had not lost a man and was well ahead of schedule. He
would be able to stop a day with Josefa at Taos; then
he would go on to meet the President of the United
States himself. Kit had passed the old copper mines
and just turned north along the Rio Grande, when he
met General Kearny and the Army of the West. The
army was barely creeping. In eleven days Kearny
had marched only a hundred and fifty miles over good
trails, but his mules were already in poor shape from
pulling the heavy army wagons which had been built
for the prairies.

In the California campaign Kit had admired Frémont greatly. It is not probable that he spared any
praise of him in telling General Kearny that the conquest of California was all finished. Kit could not
have picked a worse man to hear Frémont's praise.
Kearny was angry that this little upstart from the
Geographic Department should have the glory for the
conquest of California when that glory should right-
fully have been his. He immediately ordered Kit to
turn his dispatches over to Fitzpatrick for delivery to
the President, and to guide the Army of the West
to California.

Kit refused. He had given his word to Frémont and
Stockton that, if he lived to get through, he would
deliver the dispatches into the President's hands. He
intended to keep his word. At first Kearny tried to

persuade Kit by telling him he was superior officer to either Frémont or Stockton, and that his orders took precedence. Then he lost his temper and threatened to put Kit under arrest. This was no worry to Kit. With fifteen of his Carson Men in camp, it would be hard to hold him. He'd slip away in the night, and it would take more than two hundred dragoons to catch him.

Kit talked the matter over with Lucien Maxwell, and Lucien told him he was wrong. As a lieutenant he had to obey the orders of a general or he could be court-martialed. That was government law. Humble as Kit always was, he did want the honor of taking the dispatches to the President. But above all he wanted to do what was right and honest. Lucien knew more than he about government law. So, much as he hated to, Kit decided to obey the General's orders. What Lucien didn't know was that Kearny, an army general, had no authority over a Navy or Geographic Department officer, or over a lieutenant in the Navy Battalion of Mounted Riflemen.

12

For the United States

It is known that Kit had little respect for Kearny, either as a man or as a general. He has been accused by some writers of intentionally misleading Kearny into cutting his strength in half and causing his disaster. If that is true, it is out of character with anything Kit ever did in his life. It is also hard to believe that as stubborn a man as Kearny would let an inferior officer lead him into doing anything against his own judgment.

Kit had told Kearny that the fighting in California was ended. When he left there, it certainly had been. And he did tell Kearny that if he tried to take the wagons along he'd be all winter in reaching California. The General then transferred his supplies to mule packs and sent half his dragoons back to Santa Fe with the wagons. But he insisted on taking two mounted cannons along.

Of the march down the Gila, Dr. Griffin of the army wrote: "Every bush in this country is full of thorns, and every piece of grass, so soon as it is broken, becomes a thorn at both ends. Every rock you turn over has a tarantula or a centipede under it, and Carson says that in the summer the most beautiful specimens of rattlesnakes are scattered around in the greatest profusion. The fact is, take the country altogether, and I defy any man who has not seen it—or one as utterly worthless—even to imagine any so barren. The cactus is the only thing that does grow, and we saw some of them yesterday—I should say, fifty feet high."

Dragging the cannons over mountain passes and through narrow canyons slowed the Army of the West considerably. The troops, unused to rigors of the frontier, suffered bitterly. Many of the horses and mules died of starvation. Those that were left were little more than hide-covered skeletons. But on November 22nd Kit led the battered army out to the junction of the Gila and the Colorado rivers in what is now the very southeast corner of California.

That night campfire lights were seen across the Gila.

and Kearny sent a colonel with fifteen dragoons to investigate. A band of Mexicans with five hundred horses was found, and four of the men were taken back to camp. On being questioned by General Kearny, they said they were simply herders who were taking the horses to Sonora in Old Mexico. Kit was suspicious and wanted to hold them as prisoners, but the General was under orders to treat Mexican civilians in a friendly manner. From them he bought replacements for his worn-out horses and let them go.

Kearny's advance scouts discovered a lone peon rider the next day and brought him into camp. He was searched and found to be carrying messages from General Flores in Los Angeles to General Castro in Sonora. The messages told of the defeat of the United States forces at Los Angeles, and of the routing of 450 American soldiers and sailors who had tried to retake the town. It was evident that the war was not ended in California. Kearny pressed on across the California desert and mountains as rapidly as he could move his jaded forces. He might yet be in time to reap some of the California glory.

By December 2nd Kit had led Kearny's dragging Army of the West as far as Warner's Ranch in the mountain valley of Agua Caliente, sixty miles from San Diego. In the waterless march across the desert, all the animals except one horse and a few mules had died. The men were too exhausted to continue afoot. Here they met an English rancher who was on his way to San Diego. He told Kearny that the Mexicans, with some help from the Californios, had renewed the war in late September. They had retaken Los Angeles, but Commodore Stockton still held San Diego. Kearny sent a message by the Englishman, asking Stockton to get in touch with him at once.

While the troops were recovering, Kit heard from an Indian *vaquero* that five hundred horses had recently been sent to General Castro in Sonora for remounting his cavalry. This was the herd that Kearny had let slip by him at the Gila. The Indian also told Kit that fifteen miles to the north a smaller herd of horses was being driven to General Flores at Los Angeles. Kearny at once sent Kit and Lieutenant Davidson, with twenty-five men mounted on ranch horses, to take the nearby herd. It was taken, but many of the horses were found to be wild and unbroken.

On December 4th the captured horses that could be ridden were put under saddle, and Kearny moved his troops another fifteen miles. Nearing the little Indian village of San Pasqual the next day, he was met by Captain Gillespie and Lieutenant Beale with thirty-five men from Commodore Stockton.

Meanwhile, Kit and Captain Johnston, riding ahead with fifteen dragoons, surprised a few armed and mounted men who spurred their horses and raced away. On examining the ground, Kit discovered that the men were Californios, not Mexicans. From sign, he judged them to be pickets of a cavalry force of about a hundred and fifty and that their camp lay a few miles ahead. The Captain wanted to run the pickets down, but Kit insisted on reporting back to Kearny. He was surprised to find the Californios gathered in any such strength and suspected an ambush.

The Californios were a distinct race of people. They had originally sprung from Spanish fathers and native California Indian mothers. They were much larger than the wild Indians, far more courageous than the Mexicans, as cunning as coyotes, and among the finest horsemen on earth. During the original campaign for California, they had remained neutral, liking neither the Americans nor the Mexicans. They felt that the country west of the Sierras belonged to them but, being leaderless, had taken no action.

Kit believed the Californios had now found a leader, and that a hundred and fifty of them would be more dangerous than a thousand Mexicans. This he told Kearny. He said it looked like an ambush and recommended that the Californios be avoided, and that he lead the way to San Diego by a secret mountain pass which he knew. But Kearny was as rash as Captain Johnston had been. Zach Taylor and other generals had become famous through bold attacks in the Mexican War, and Kearny was hungry for fame. He determined to attack as soon as he found the exact position of the enemy camp.

Kearny blamed Kit for having told him the war was ended in California, and causing him to send half his troops back to Santa Fe. It is evident that he now distrusted both Kit and his judgment. Instead of sending him to do the scouting, he sent Lieutenant Hammond with a small party and a native Indian guide. Hammond fumbled the assignment, was seen and challenged by the Californio pickets, and returned to camp at two o'clock in the morning. Kearny then decided to make his attack at daybreak.

The Californios' camp was seemingly surprised at breakfast. The cavalrymen leaped on their excellent horses and raced away, each man carrying a long pole. Captain Johnston waved his sword and shouted for the attack.

As Kit had suspected, Kearny was being led into an ambush. The Californios, on far superior mounts, kept just beyond gunshot until the dragoons were strung out in a line a quarter of a mile long. Then, suddenly breaking ranks, they wheeled and came racing back to meet the charging Americans. Extended in front of each rider was his long pole and attached to its end was a razor-sharp lance. Before the dragoons could raise their rifles, the lances mowed them down like sickles cutting through dry grass. It was over in less than two minutes.

As the cannons rumbled into sight, the Californios again wheeled their horses and spurred away. The ground was littered with dead, dying and wounded. Of the forty Americans who had reached the front, thirty-six had been killed or seriously wounded. Kit's life was probably saved because his horse stumbled and fell. Kearny himself had been wounded twice and was bleeding heavily. There was nothing to do but make camp on the spot, try to save the wounded, and bury the dead.

The situation of the Army of the West was not good. The Californios ringed the hill, just out of rifle range. Without water the wounded were dying like poisoned flies. The thirsty animals fought to break away and find water, and there was nothing to eat except raw mule meat. At night Kearny sent messengers for help from Commodore Stockton, but they were captured within sight of the camp.

With most of his officers killed, Kearny placed Kit in command of fifteen men the next day, and ordered an advance to the nearest water. The Californios again attacked. The mules pulling one of the cannons ran away and were captured by the enemy, and the Army of the West was forced onto another dry hill. As dusk settled, the Californios taunted Kearny, shouted to ask why he didn't send other messengers, waved their lances, and made signs with their hands as if cutting a throat.　.

Now the situation was desperate. Unless help could be brought from Commodore Stockton within three days, no man in the command would remain alive. And none but the most skillful and daring messenger could hope to get through that tight ring of Californio lances. Kit knew it must be he and stepped forward to volunteer. Beside him Lieutenant Beale stepped forward, to be followed by an Indian boy who was his admiring servant.

In the first dark of night, the three messengers slithered from the camp like snakes. Behind, the camp was as still as death. The stillness warned the Californios. From a few yards down the hill, a voice rang out, *"Tenga cuidad! Se escapará el lobo!"* (Be careful! The wolf will escape!) It was clear that the Californios knew Kit was in the camp and expected him to be the messenger. Beale's shoe scraped a rock, there was a clatter of hoofs, and a sentry pulled his horse to a stop within a few feet of Kit's head. Beale pressed against his side in the blackness. With his mouth close to Kit's ear, he whispered, "We're gone."

"No," Kit whispered back. "I been in worse places afore, and Providence saved me." Providence saved them then. After a minute or two the sentry rode on. Kit couldn't risk another scraped rock. He had the canteens abandoned and the men's shoes tied to the backs of their belts. Bleeding and burning from thousands of cactus spines in their flesh, the three men crawled on for two miles. When they dared climb to their feet, the shoes had been lost from their belts. It was forty miles to San Diego through rough, cactus-spattered, enemy territory; and every step would have to be taken barefooted in darkness. They made it during the second night, but Beale was brought in delirious from cactus poisoning and fatigue.

A hundred armed sailors and eighty marines were sent at once to rescue Kearny and what was left of his Army of the West. On sight of the reinforcements, the Californios withdrew. Travois were made to carry those unable to walk, and slowly the disabled army was moved into San Diego.

Lieutenant Beale went insane from the hardships of the daring adventure, and it was two years before he fully recovered. For a while it was believed that Kit would lose both feet, but his excellent physical condition saved them. In two months he was as well as ever.

In the meantime, General Kearny had recovered and, in spite of his disaster with the Army of the West, declared himself the Supreme Military Commander of California. He ordered Commodore Stockton and Governor Frémont to obey his commands, but they showed him no respect and refused to recognize his authority.

The situation went from bad to worse. On February 25, 1847, Frémont again sent Kit to Washington with dispatches. This time he met President Polk. The President liked Kit very much and appointed him a second lieutenant of Mounted Riflemen in the United States Army. Then he sent him back to California with dispatches for, "whoever might be senior military officer when he got there."

When Kit reached California in October, he found none of the military officers he had known. Kearny had placed Frémont under arrest on a charge of treason and had taken him east for court-martial. All the old band, including Kit's Carson Men, had been discharged without pay and had scattered. Colonel Mason was Military Governor, and his adjutant was a young lieutenant named William Tecumseh Sherman. Kit and Sherman became close friends. In the spring Kit was again sent to Washington with dispatches.

When Kit reached Santa Fe on June 14, 1848, the first news he heard was that the Senate had refused to approve his appointment as a lieutenant in the U. S. Army. It had also failed to approve payment of the men who had been in Frémont's service. For three years Kit had been in government service of the most dangerous kind. He had saved the lives of both Kearny and Frémont, spent all his capital, gone in debt for Josefa's living expenses, and would not receive one cent of pay for it or one word of thanks. It was evident that Kearny had influenced the Senate and was striking at Frémont and all those who had been loyal to him.

Kit's friends urged him to quit immediately and to turn his dispatches over to the government officer at Santa Fe. It took Kit less than a minute to give them his answer. "I didn't ask for no army commission; the President give it to me. I didn't do what I done for Kearny, or for the Senate, or for pay; I done it for the United States. The job ain't finished till I get these here dispatches fetched clean through to Washington."

13

Father Kit of the Utes

During the California campaign, several of the Carson Men had been killed, and most of the rest had scattered. When Kit returned from taking the dispatches east, there was no way for him to make a living in Taos. The previous year the Taos Pueblo Indians had revolted. Goaded by the local priest, they had joined with Mexicans in an attempt to drive out the Americans. Although the revolt failed, many Americans were killed and much property was destroyed. Among those killed was Governor Charles Bent, Kit's friend and brother-in-law.

Shortly before Kit had married Josefa, Lucien Maxwell married the daughter of Don Carlos Beaubien. Don Carlos had died, and his ranch had been inherited by Lucien. It was larger than the entire state of Delaware. Lucien wanted only one man for a ranching partner, and that man was Kit Carson.

For five years Kit and Lucien tried to raise cattle and horses profitably, but ranching in New Mexico in those days was rugged business. Thousands of American settlers had moved across the Missouri onto fertile farm lands in the central west. Those lands had been given to the Indians, to be theirs forever; but the treaty was scrapped, and the tribes were being driven into the arid prairies south of the Arkansas River.

With the buffalo rapidly disappearing, the Utes, Kiowas, Apaches, Arapahos, Cheyennes and Navajos were finding it easier to raid ranches than to hunt game on the land the settlers didn't want. Kit and Maxwell gathered the few remaining Carson Men around them. There was hardly a month when they didn't have to fight one Indian tribe or another, and more of the men were killed in these battles.

The United States sent in a few companies of cavalry to control the Indians, but they were almost useless. Their officers knew nothing of Indians, could seldom track down marauders, often took out their spite on the innocent, and generally did more harm than

The Indians made frequent raids on the ranches.

good. A few Indian agencies were set up, but the agents were always political appointees. Usually they were aged easterners, worse than the cavalry officers. Though Kit had sworn he would have nothing more to do with the army, he was continually called upon to act as scout or guide—and he always went. A great deal of his time was lost from his ranching, and he was never paid for his services. But he felt it was his duty to see that the guilty Indians were punished and that the innocent were left in peace.

Though he was seldom there, Kit had established Josefa in a good home on the ranch by 1853, had brought Adaline back from St. Louis, and was raising a family. But he wasn't getting ahead. Continual Indian raids had made ranching unprofitable. At this time Kit and Lucien went into the sheep droving business. The California gold rush, which had been on for four years, was petering out, and the miners were turning to ranching. Word reached Kit that sheep were scarce in California and were selling for more than five dollars a head. In southern New Mexico, the Rio Grande Valley was swarming with sheep. A man could buy them for a dollar apiece.

It is probable that Lucien lent Kit the money, but in any event, each bought sixty-five hundred sheep. To have driven them to California across the southwestern deserts or along the Gila River would have been impossible. The Navajos were gathering in large bands and raiding as far south as Old Mexico. Livestock which they took in these raids was driven into the gulches and canyons of the high mesas. It was as completely lost as if it had evaporated.

With Kit leading the way, he and Maxwell drove their flocks north to the Oregon Trail, over the South Pass, and followed the route Kit had pioneered for Frémont across the Great Basin. The drive of nearly two thousand miles was made with very few losses, and Kit's sheep sold for $5.50 a head. It was Kit's first really big fortune, and for the rest of his life he was independent. After visiting old friends in California, he and Lucien returned to Taos by way of the Gila River. On the way, they met the Mormon delegate to Congress, and from him Kit heard that he had been appointed Indian Agent at Taos. He reached home on Christmas Day, 1853, and took up his new job at the first of the year.

In the May after Kit became Indian Agent, Congress created the territories of Kansas and Nebraska. More thousands of settlers poured into the new territories, and Indian resentment against the whites rose sharply. To make matters worse, escaped convicts, thugs, and outlaws of every description were pouring into the West. There the laws were few and the enforcement agencies fewer.

From the time of Kit's first report as Indian Agent at Taos, it was plain that he was as determined to protect the Indians from the whites as to protect the whites from the Indians. Many Indian agencies were being set up throughout the West. Agents came and agents went, but Kit outlasted them all. In spite of numerous political changes in governors, Presidents, and top officers in the United States Indian Agency, he remained in his post as agent for the Utes and Jicarilla Apaches until the outbreak of the Civil War.

Though Kit had to hire a clerk to write for him, his reports for those seven years are still on file, and the same demands are made in all of them:

"There must be laws to stop white men from furnishing liquor to Indians."

"The Indian has always lived by the chase. You have taken away all his good hunting grounds. He is starving, and it is your responsibility to feed him."

"It is cheaper to feed starving Indians than to let them raid the ranches and settlements of the whites. If you do not feed them, you cannot stop their raiding."

"Indians are not farmers by instinct and heredity; they are hunters. Their hunting grounds have

been taken away from them and their game need-
lessly slaughtered. If they are ever again to be
self-supporting, they must be given fertile land
and tools, and taught to raise crops. Grown Indian men cannot be taught to farm, but if the
boys are gathered on reservations and put under
good farmers, in twenty years the American Indian will again be self-supporting."

"There were few bad Indians before the white
man took away their means of gaining a living.
There are still many more good Indians than bad
ones. There must be laws in the territories to protect good Indians from bad whites, and enough
troops to enforce the laws. Bad Indians must be
punished, regardless of cost, or all Indians will become bad. Troops being sent to punish Indians
must be led by officers who know and understand
Indians."

Kit practiced what he preached. When a white man
in his district injured an Indian, he had Kit Carson to
deal with, and that dealing was sharp and to the point.
In order that the troops in his district might have leadership that knew and understood Indians, Kit became
a volunteer officer, and spent more than half his time
acting as scout and tracker for the cavalry. While other
agents required whole Indian sub-tribes to come to

their offices for dealing—often more than a hundred miles—Kit rode to deal with them in their own villages.

It was dangerous to have Indians come to the settlements and learn the bad habits of the whites. Proof of Kit's wisdom in handling the Indians is clearly shown in the records of the Office of Indian Affairs in Washington. During his term as their agent, his Utes and Apaches were peaceful. On all sides the other tribes were continually going on the warpath. The Apaches called him "Kit," but among the Utes he was "Father Kit."

At the outbreak of the Civil War, there was probably no man who had performed greater service for the United States Army and received less recognition than Kit Carson. In the previous eighteen years, he had devoted more than half his time, had ridden many thousand miles, and risked his life hundreds of times without one cent of pay. Even the lieutenancy given him by President Polk had been taken away. Most of our frontiersmen, like Kit himself, had come from states which had joined the rebellion. All his brothers had hurried to join the Rebel Army. Throughout the West, cavalry officers were resigning their commands and going to join the side of the Confederacy. They reminded Kit of the injustices done him by the Senate and the Army of the United States, and urged him to go with them. His answer was the same as it had been when his lieutenancy was taken away: "I wa'n't a-doin' it for neither the Senate nor the Army. I was a-doin' it for the United States, and I still aim to."

14

Canyon de Chelly

At the outbreak of the Civil War, only eight men could be found to raise the Stars and Stripes above the plaza in Taos, and Kit Carson was one of the eight. As soon as President Lincoln called for volunteers, Kit resigned as Indian Agent. With Colonel St. Vrain, he organized the First New Mexico Volunteer Infantry, and was appointed lieutenant colonel. St. Vrain was too old to stand army life and soon resigned. Kit was appointed colonel in his place, and by army standards, was a poor officer. Most of his troops and many of his officers were shiftless, lazy, Mexican peons. Kit had no interest in spit-and-polish, but he taught his men to shoot the antiquated rifles furnished them, toughened their bodies, and taught them to obey commands.

The only Civil War engagement of Kit's volunteers was in the Battle of Valverde on February 12, 1862. The Texans were driving up the Rio Grande to New Mexico. They were met at Valverde by a force of the U. S. Army under Colonel Canby. Twenty-five companies of New Mexico Volunteers were sent to support Canby, and eight of these companies were under Kit's command. The battle resulted in a Union defeat, largely because most of the Mexican Volunteers became frightened under fire, would not obey orders, and ran away.

Kit's eight companies were the only ones of the twenty-five to fight bravely. He was ordered to cross the river at the right of the artillery, and to use his troops as skirmishers to cut off an enemy flanking attack. This was Kit's kind of fighting, and the kind for which he had trained his troops. Slithering through the tall grass and brush like Indians, they were cutting a swath through the Texas flankers. Suddenly from far behind them the Union bugles sounded retreat.

Kit was sure he was in the midst of a glorious victory. His troops had gained a half mile beyond the river. What was this? Some more blundering by those Regular Army officers? What were they blowing retreat for when they had the battle almost won? Kit was boiling mad as he led his troops back across the river. It was several days before he could understand that, in battle, an entire force must fight as a single unit, and that the commanding officer must consider the position of his whole force. The lesson later saved him from the fate that Custer suffered at Little Bighorn.

In spite of the showing of Kit's troops, the Battle of Valverde proved the worthlessness of Mexican volunteer soldiers under fire. With the cavalry withdrawn from the prairies to fight in the war, there was little control over the Indians. The Utes and Apaches who had been under Kit's care remained loyal. Most of the other tribes of the Southwest went on the warpath, raiding, murdering and plundering the whites. The New Mexico Volunteers were withdrawn from the war and set to fighting Indians. Even in this Kit found himself handicapped. He was obliged to take his orders from army officers, and they were too busy with the war to pay much attention to Indians. Often Kit's troops were ordered to camp and were left for months with nothing to do and with no rations. Kit made use of this time by learning to read and write.

Among all the Indian tribes, the Navajos were the most difficult to control. For generations they had lived among the deep canyons of the high mesa country of western New Mexico. They had no great chief, as the other Indian tribes had, but were divided into family tribes. A treaty made with the chief of one tribe was not binding on the others. Their homeland covered many thousands of square miles of waterless desert. Unlike other Indians, they were farmers. Where there was fertile land in the deep canyons, they raised grain, had peach orchards, and kept sheep, goats, cattle and horses. The number of Navajos had always depended on the amount of food they could raise or steal from their neighbors. With the start of the Civil War, the Navajos prospered. Their raiding parties spread in every direction. The plunder disappeared into the canyons which they alone knew, and was lost forever.

The War Department had sent three large expeditions under high-ranking generals to punish the Navajos, but they had all failed. They wore their armies to shreds and lost their animals and equipment in the deserts. They could never find more than a handful of Navajos. Those that were found fought like wolves and ripped formations of soldiers to pieces. Then they retreated into the maze of canyons and were soon lost. After the third failure of the army, Kit was ordered to take the Navajos off their homeland, and confine them on a small reservation in eastern New Mexico.

For years Kit had been writing the Department of Indian Affairs that the Indians should be put on reservations and taught modern farming. He had now been given the job of carrying out his own recommendation.

As he saw it, it was not his business to kill the Navajos, but simply to move them. He went about it in a way that would save the most lives. Instead of hunting down the Indians, he hunted down their crops and herds.

After setting up patrols to stop Navajo raids on their neighbors, Kit began to destroy the food supply in their homeland. All through the summer and fall of 1863, he spread his raiding parties over thousands of square miles of the high mesa country. They sought out hundreds of remote valleys and canyons, destroyed the standing grain in the fields, cut down orchards, and seized sheep, cattle and horses.

When testifying before a Congressional Indian Commission in 1865, Kit said, "When I captured the Navajos, I first destroyed their crops, and harassed them until the snow fell very deep in the canyons, taking some prisoners occasionally. . . . I took twelve hundred sheep from them at one time, and smaller lots at different times. . . . It took me and three hundred men most of one day to destroy a field of corn."

Deep in the Navajo country, in eastern Arizona, is the Canyon de Chelly (de Shay). The name is taken from the Navajo word, *tseyi*, which means "among the cliffs." The canyon, lying below the surface of the mesa, is about thirty miles long. Its straight cliff walls rise more than a thousand feet above the valley floor. For unknown generations, Canyon de Chelly had been the impregnable fortress of the Navajos. They alone knew the secret passages up the cliffs. There, two hundred feet above the narrow valley floor, they had their permanent fortifications which could not be reached by rifle or cannon fire. From these they could rain down arrows and heavy boulders on an invading enemy. Colonel Sumner and General Canby had each chased the Navajos into Canyon de Chelly in previous attempts to conquer them, but both had been forced to withdraw hurriedly.

With the coming of winter in 1863, many of the Navajos forted up in the canyon. Kit's scouts reported that there was no large movement of Indians, but they were drifting into the canyon in small parties. Kit bided his time and laid his plans. The Navajo strategy was clear to him. The chiefs were trying to trick him into an attack within the canyon. If he should take his whole force between those impregnable walls, his troops could be cut off from escape and massacred.

While he had been a trapper in the mountains, Kit had learned that it was often wise to use the same strategy against the Indians that they were trying to use against him. If the Navajos were planning to trap him in the Canyon de Chelly, why not reverse the play and trap them?

It was twenty-five miles from Kit's main camp to the western portal of the great canyon, and about twice as far to its eastern end. He waited until there was a deep fall of snow, which would make the narrow shelves on the cliff walls treacherous for Indian maneuvers. Then, on January 6, 1864, he sent Captain Pfeiffer with about a hundred men to shut off escape at the eastern portal. Next day he moved his main camp to plug the western exit. It took five days to move the camp by ox teams through the deep snow.

Meanwhile, with Sergeant Herrera, Kit methodically scouted both sides of the canyon from the rim and stationed soldiers to cut off escape from any side exits. He did not try to keep his troops concealed but let the Navajos see what he was doing. It was his plan to strengthen his force at the eastern portal, then send a small detachment through the canyon. He did not think the Indians would attack the detachment, when their fighting shelves were clogged by snow, and when they knew they were cut off from escape.

Captain Pfeiffer reached the eastern portal before the slow-moving main camp had closed the portal on the western end. He was an impatient, and sometimes reckless, officer. Without waiting for reinforcements or orders from Kit, he started his march through the Canyon de Chelly on January 12th. Fortunately Kit had been right in his belief that the Navajos would not make a direct attack. From their fortified positions high along the cliff sides, they shouted curses and insults at the soldiers, but they kept out of rifle range.

The march through the canyon took two days, and

there was not a man lost. In making his report, Captain Pfeiffer wrote: "At the place where I encamped (the night of January 12th) the curl of smoke from my fires ascended to where a large body of Indians were resting over my head, but the height was so great that the Indians did not look larger than crows, and as we were too far apart to injure each other, no damage was done except with the tongue."

This was the first march of soldiers through the canyon which had been thought to be impregnable. As planned, it was more of an exploration than an attack on the fortress. During the march Captain Pfeiffer discovered that in places the floor of the canyon was wide and very fertile. There were more than two thousand peach trees in the valley, rich pastures, and large fields where corn and wheat had been raised. This was what Kit wanted to know. He sent a larger force back through the canyon, with orders to avoid a battle if possible, but to destroy the orchards and capture animals which the Indians might use for food.

Kit's strategy worked well. In making his next report on the Navajo campaign, General Carleton, Kit's commanding officer, wrote: "Results of this expedition: Indians killed, twenty-three; wounded, five; prisoners, thirty-four; voluntarily surrendered, two hundred; and two hundred head of sheep and goats captured."

With the forcing of their great natural stronghold and with the destruction of their orchards, the Navajos realized they were beaten. By February 4th, a thousand of them had voluntarily surrendered. By the middle of the month, thirty-five hundred had given themselves up and been sent away to the reservation. There were not believed to be more than six thousand Navajos in all the tribes. By April 10th, more than eight thousand had come in from their food-stripped homeland, had given themselves up, and had been moved to the reservation.

15

The Battle of Adobe Walls

Though Kit had taken the Navajos from their homeland, he had done it with such care that they still respected and admired him. He was sent to administer their new reservation, but it was a failure because the land was worthless and the government failed to supply proper equipment or food. The Civil War was nearing its end. Kit's old injury—one he had suffered when his horse fell with him in the mountains while he was Indian Agent—was becoming very painful. And he was lonesome for his home and family. He petitioned his commanding officer for a release from the service.

The petition was denied. While Kit had been busy with the Navajos, the plains Indians had gone entirely out of control. They were no longer trying to hunt for a living. Instead they were growing fat and wealthy from raids on the trail caravans, the ranches, and the settlements. It was feared there would be a united uprising of all the Indians west of the Missouri River.

William Bent had been sent to distribute presents among the Cheyennes and Arapahos and to try to make a peace treaty with them. This enraged the Kiowas, Kiowa Apaches and Comanches. They said they were being punished for being good and set to work to show how bad they could be. The period of enlistment of most of the Volunteers had expired. There were not enough soldiers in New Mexico to go against the plains Indians. In August, 1864, Kit was asked to raise a force of Utes and Navajos to fight the Kiowas, Kiowa Apaches and Comanches.

Kit sent back word that the Navajos would not fight the plains Indians, and that he didn't believe it necessary to fight them at all. He was sure he could make peace with those tribes if he could go among them with such presents as those given the Cheyennes and Arapahos. Before the red tape could be untangled and presents provided, there were further outrages. In October

General Carleton promised Kit two hundred volunteer soldiers and a hundred friendly Indians, and ordered him to go against the Kiowas, Kiowa Apaches and Comanches. They were reported to be in their winter camps along Palo Duro Creek, in what is now the panhandle of Texas.

During Kit's years as Indian Agent, he had noticed that the plains Indians were gathering in ever larger winter camps. Where a single tribe had once wintered in several widely separated camps, they were beginning to set their villages close together. Sometimes two or three entirely different tribes would winter in a single valley. Kit didn't believe a force of three hundred would be strong enough to go against the three tribes if camped close together. This he told to General Carleton, and asked to be supported by a strong force of Regular Army dragoons and at least two mounted howitzers.

The nearest strong force of Regular Army cavalry was at Fort Larned, Kansas, under General Blunt. Carleton was General of Volunteers and did not like to call upon the Regular Army for help. He felt that Kit was overcautious, that howitzers would be useless against Indians, and that the regular cavalry was unnecessary. When Kit insisted, the General reluctantly agreed. He said he would send word to Blunt, asking him to attack Palo Duro from the east in late November. He would let Kit know the exact time of Blunt's attack, so that both forces might strike at the same moment.

Kit was to meet his troops at Fort Bascom on November 10th. He was still worried about going against the plains Indians with so small a force, and took with him sixty-five picked Ute warriors who were his friends. When he reached the fort, he found that General Carleton had sent him 321 volunteers, fourteen officers, and two mounted howitzers. One of the officers brought word that General Blunt would strike Palo Duro Creek at sunrise on November 26th, that the Indian winter camp had been scouted, and that its strength was not great.

It was two hundred miles from Fort Bascom to Palo Duro, and Kit advanced as rapidly as his supply train could be moved, keeping Ute scouts well out ahead and on both sides. At sunset on November 24th—the second nationally established Thanksgiving Day—Kit's little army made camp on the Canadian River, thirty miles west of a deserted trading post that had been known as Adobe Walls. Palo Duro Creek was still nearly two days' march away. If Kit was to have his troops there, rested and ready to attack with Blunt at sunrise on the twenty-sixth, he would have to march all night.

Leaving his supply train to follow the next morning,

Kit mounted 246 men and thirteen officers at dusk. With the howitzers at the rear of his forces, he marched down the valley of the Canadian River. In the first gray of dawn, one of the Ute scouts saw a mounted Indian race away down the river. There was no question in Kit's mind. This was a Kiowa sentry, but he could not be from the main camp. That was on Palo Duro Creek, well to the south. Ahead were Paladora Creek and the ruins of Adobe Walls. A small Kiowa camp must be near the old trading post, and it must be captured before word of the coming attack could be taken to the main Indian winter camp. Experience had taught Kit that surprise was the best weapon to use in an Indian attack. With a shout he sent his troops racing after the Kiowa.

On they raced through the tall dry grass and brush of the river bottom, the Kiowa sentry streaking ahead. Within a mile they came upon a large herd of stolen horses and cattle. Superb horsemen, the Utes dashed into the milling herd, sprang from their tired ponies onto the best of the stolen band, and raced on in the lead. The crumbling remains of Adobe Walls came into sight on a rise of ground near the river. Just beyond, the first streaks of sunlight gleamed on the whitened buffalo hide of more than a hundred and fifty Kiowa teepees. The war whooping of the Utes had given warning of the attack. The squaws and papooses had run to hide in the bushes, and the braves had caught up their rifles, powder horns and war ponies.

As Kit spurred his buckskin pacer toward the abandoned trading post, he took in the whole picture at a glance. A few hundred yards beyond the sagging Adobe Walls, 400 Kiowa warriors were fighting their fractious horses, and slowly retreating eastward down the valley. These were no bow-and-arrow Indians, and they were mounted on no scrawny Indian ponies. The Kiowas were rich from the plundering of caravans. Every brave was mounted on a fine war horse. From the gleam of the sun on steel, Kit knew their rifles were newer and better than those carried by his ill-equipped volunteers. The Kiowas were sneaks and thieves, but they were never cowards. No Kiowa would run to save his own life, and abandon his squaw, his children and his teepee. Something was wrong here. The Indians were trying to lead him into an ambush. Swinging his horse toward the top of a low hill, Kit reined in and shouted, "Blow halt!" to the bugler beside him.

Whipping out his field glass, Kit trained it on the milling band of Kiowa warriors. It had been ten years since he had seen them, but he recognized the chiefs. There was Dohasan, great war chief of the Kiowas, Set-imka, and Satanta—terror of all the plains and master of the slashing, whirlwind attack. This was no small winter camp; the whole Kiowa nation was close by. Someone had blundered and confused Palo Duro with Paladora Creek. There would be no help from Blunt and his cavalry.

Even in the few seconds that Kit had trained his glass, Dohasan sensed that his ambush attempt had failed. Swinging his arm, he bellowed a command. Setimka and Satanta wheeled their horses, swung their rifles above their heads, and formed their braves for the charge.

There was no moment in which to form a plan of battle. In less than a minute, four hundred frenzied Kiowas would be ripping through Kit's unformed, winded ranks, tearing them to shreds and scattering them for slaughter. No man without Kit Carson's mountain training and natural instinct could have prepared to meet that charge. Above the trample and din, his usually quiet voice cut like a skinning knife. "Wheel them cannons about! Load with ball! Fire! Officers for'ards!"

Kiowas and Kiowa horses knew rifle fire and were not afraid to face it, but the mighty roar of the mountain howitzers caught them in mid-charge and threw them into panic. As the braves brought their rearing mounts under control, they sat spellbound, staring at the cloud of smoke rising from the hillside. Then they withdrew for a council.

Kit knew the battle was far from won. Dohasan

would soon discover that the howitzers had done no great damage, and the troops were between the Kiowas and their village. It would be only minutes before they would charge again. Kit's horses, trail-worn from twenty-four hours under saddle, would go down like prairie dogs before the Kiowa attack. Without horses there would be no possibility of retreat. Calling his officers about him, Kit gave his commands in short, quick sentences. "Git all mounts inside the old fort walls! Spread all hands out to skirmish in the high grass! Powder's short; don't nobody shoot till his sights is on an Injun! Git both them cannons a-top the hill! Officers, hold your men even roundabouts! Watch out for attack from the rear!"

Again and again the Kiowas charged. Kit stood between the two howitzers at the brow of the hill. Waiting until the charging horde was almost upon his position, he snapped out his orders: "Number one, *fire!* Number two, *fire!*" The volleys from the howitzers split each charge. But the Indians swept on around the hill, lying flat on their horses' neck and pouring lead into the position. After each sweep they withdrew to reload and reform for another charge.

Within the first hour reinforcements began joining the Kiowas. Between charges Kit studied the bands with his field glass. From their war paint he could recognize Comanches and Kiowa Apaches. He sighted

The Indian war chief was setting fire to the dry grass.

his glass far down the valley to the east. What he saw would have brought despair to any other commander. The floor of the valley was swarming with advancing Indians. Beyond them was a village of more than three hundred wigwams. This was no ordinary winter camp of any tribe. This was a long-planned ambush. The tribes of the plains had gathered to teach the white man a lesson—to drive him from their homeland.

As more Comanches and Kiowa Apaches joined the attack, their fresh ponies were stampeded by the roar of the howitzers, and the charges became confused. By mid-afternoon at least four thousand naked, whooping, shooting Indians were continually racing their ponies through the high grass around Kit's position. Blue powder smoke filled the air. Though thousands of shots were being fired into the position, little damage was being done by the Indians. Fear of the howitzers held them away from the base of the hill, and made them perfect targets for the Utes and troopers skirmishing in the tall grass.

Late in the afternoon Dohasan sent the lesser chiefs to withdraw their tribesmen from the attack. This was the move Kit had feared. The crafty old chief had worked out a more effective plan of battle. Presently, wisps of smoke rose from the throng of Indians gathered around Dohasan. If the old chief had shouted his plan to Kit, he could not have understood it better.

The tall grass and brush surrounding the hill and extending nearly to its dome were as dry as tinder, and a breeze was rising. Dohasan was going to set fire to the grass. In the freshening afternoon breeze, the whole hill would quickly become a raging bonfire in which no man could live.

Instantly Kit saw both his danger and his advantage. The breeze was from the west. To burn the hill, the Indians would have to circle the position and set their fires to the west of it. This would give Kit time to withdraw his forces. If the breeze continued to freshen, he could whip the Indians with their own weapon. Swinging his glass, he searched out a position to the south where the grass was so short that a fire could be controlled.

Indians with flaming firebrands were racing up the valley between Kit and the river as he shouted his orders for the retreat. Behind the cover of dense smoke that rolled ahead of the flames, Kit moved his troops and mounts to their new position without a single loss. He was no sooner away from the path of the flames than he called his Utes to him. He must act quickly while Dohasan thought him to be trapped on the burning hill. Speaking to the Utes in their own language, he sent them running to spread the fire the entire width of the valley.

Fanned by the freshening breeze, a mile-wide line of

flames was soon sweeping eastward through the dry grass like a giant scythe. Before it, four thousand Kiowa, Kiowa Apache, and Comanche warriors rode for their lives.

Kit knew his advantage was only temporary and that the greatest danger still lay ahead. Soon the Indians would stop the fire by burning off a wide swath in its path. Then they would be back, shrieking for revenge. If they caught him on burned-over ground with no cover for his skirmishers, his whole troop would be massacred at the first charge. Worse than that, he didn't know where his supply train might be. If the Indians captured it, they would have had a great victory.

It was two hundred miles to the nearest settlement, across a barren, lifeless desert. Without supplies, few of the troops could be saved. The train must be found and reached before the Indians discovered and captured it. But before retreating, he must give these Indians all the punishment he could. He ordered that the Kiowa village be searched for white prisoners and burned as quickly as possible.

The Kiowa village had 176 teepees, and they were all loaded with plunder from caravans and settlements. Though no white prisoners were found, there was evidence that many had been taken and held. White women's and children's clothing, photographs, letters and trinkets were in many of the teepees. Even parts of U. S. Cavalry uniforms were found, together with large quantities of trade goods, blankets and food. One large teepee was set aside as the royal livery stable. There were several sets of harness and a buggy which was used as Dohasan's royal coach.

It was nearly sunset when the first Indians broke through the fire wall and came racing back up the burned-out valley. Kit began his slow and careful retreat, keeping his troops well grouped and awaiting nightfall. With the first darkness, he must get his Ute scouts out to search for the supply train. Until then his retreat must be as slow as possible so that, if the supply train were near at hand, it might not be discovered by the attackers.

As night settled, the Indians pressed their attack so closely that Kit was unable to send out the Utes. With the last light dying from the sky, he searched the western horizon for the most defensible route of retreat. Far to his right a tiny speck of light flickered, then disappeared. Again there was a flicker. Then three or four specks twinkled like distant fireflies. These could only be the campfires of the supply train, and their twinkling was caused by the teamsters moving around them to cook their suppers. The firing was increased at the rear, to attract and hold the Indians' attention. Ute runners were sent to the supply train with word to put out the campfires. By midnight Kit had made his retreat in such a way as to meet and surround his supply train. Before dawn the Indians had withdrawn.

Against far better equipment than that of his troops, and outnumbered ten to one, Kit had withstood an almost constant Indian attack for nearly eighteen hours. A large number of attackers had been killed, but Kit had lost only a half dozen killed and twenty-five wounded. When, after breakfast, he ordered his troops to saddle and continue the retreat, his officers were surprised and displeased. They argued that only one of the Indian villages had been destroyed, and that fifty Indians had been killed for each trooper lost. Why run away from a battle that was being won?

Kit had learned the difference between a winning and losing battle at Valverde. He had been licked in good shape by the plains Indians, and he knew it. What he didn't know was that he had performed one of the most difficult of all military tactics—that of a defeated commander withdrawing his troops successfully when under heavy fire of a greatly superior force. If Kit Carson had listened to his own officers, or rushed into the ambush originally set for him, there is no doubt that his entire force would have been massacred within a few minutes.

In almost exactly the same situation as Kit's, General Custer made the mistake of boldly attacking the

Sioux Indians twelve years later at the Little Bighorn. Custer became a national hero for his failure. Carson's brilliant success is almost unknown. A national monument has been erected on the site of Custer's battle on the Little Bighorn, but the prairie wind blows sand around the crumbled ruins of Adobe Walls.

16

Adios, Compadre

When Kit had successfully withdrawn his troops to Fort Bascom, he made his report to General Carleton. He said it would require 700 additional mounted troops, four cannon, and four months' supplies in order to defeat the allied tribes of plains Indians. The General was unable to raise the needed reinforcements. In notifying Kit to disband his forces at the end of 1864, General Carleton wrote of the Battle of Adobe Walls, "This brilliant affair adds another green leaf to the laurel wreath which you have so nobly won in the service of your country."

Kit's old injury was giving him trouble, and he asked to be retired with the disbanding of his troops. But his friend, General Carleton, urged him to remain. On January 30, 1865, Carleton again wrote Kit:

"Colonel: I received your letter from Fort Union, and it gratifies me to learn that you will not leave the service while I remain here. A great deal of my good fortune in Indian matters—in fact, nearly all with reference to the Navajos, Mescalero Apaches, and Kiowas—is due to you, and it affords me pleasure always to acknowledge the value of your services."

It is evident that Kit's worth was now recognized not only by General Carleton, but by the War Department in Washington. On March 13, 1865, he was brevetted Brigadier General of Volunteers, "for gallantry in the battle of Valverde, and for distinguished service in New Mexico."

The confidence and trust which the Indians of the Southwest had in Kit Carson were as well recognized in Washington as his ability in military matters. Immediately after being made a brigadier general, Kit was called to serve with a Special Joint Congressional Committee, appointed by order of President Lincoln as an Indian treaty commission. Kit spent almost the whole year of 1865 in parleys and meetings with the same tribes of plains Indians that he had fought at Adobe

Walls. Their respect and confidence in him were so great that in October of that year friendship treaties were signed with the Apaches, Kiowas, Comanches, Arapahos and Cheyennes.

Ever since the Battle of Adobe Walls, Kit had suffered with severe pain in his throat and chest. During the year with the commission, a cough developed, he often raised blood, and was feeling "porely," as he described it. When, in April, 1866, General Carleton was mustered out of the Volunteer Service, Kit felt he had fulfilled his promise and should now be allowed to retire. For more than twenty years, he had longed for a home and family. Now that he had them, he was never able to live with them. He was sick, and he wanted to go home where Josefa could take care of him.

While serving with the Indian Treaty Commission, Kit again met William Tecumseh Sherman, now one of the great generals of the Civil War; and their friendship was renewed. This time it was General Sherman who urged Kit to remain in the service. The Ute Indians of the Rockies were on the point of an uprising against the prospectors who were swarming through the mountains in the wild search for gold. The U. S. government had made treaties with the Utes in which it had promised to keep the whites out of the Indian's hunting grounds in the mountains, but the government could not control the prospectors, and the treaties had become worthless scraps of paper. Reporting to General Sherman regarding the Utes in August, 1866, Major General John Pope wrote: "I need not say that Carson is the best man in the country to control these Indians and prevent war if it can be done. He is personally known and liked by every Indian of the bands likely to make trouble. . . . Peace with these Indians is of all things desirable, and no man is so certain to insure it as Kit Carson."

Much as Kit wanted to return to Taos, the Utes were his friends and they needed him. They had been "Father Kit's Indians" during his seven years as Indian Agent at Taos, and he could not sit back and see them drawn into a war which would surely destroy them. He accepted General Sherman's appointment as commander at Fort Garland, in the southern mountain country of Colorado Territory. The fort was built of logs, with adobe houses, and into one of these Kit moved Josefa and the children.

During his year and a half at Fort Garland, Kit's health grew steadily worse. He could no longer ride a horse, but he often made long trips into the mountains in a litter swung between two mules. No matter what the distance might be, or how rough the trail, he insisted on going to deal with the Ute chiefs in their own lodges.

By November, 1867, Kit's health was so poor that he could no longer command Fort Garland, and the need for his being there seemed past. Ouray, the head chief of the Uncompahgre Utes, had become Kit's warm friend. Under him the Ute Nation was at peace with the whites. On November 22, 1867, Kit was mustered out of the service, and the New Mexico Volunteers were forever disbanded.

It often happens that the most brilliant acts of a man's life go almost unnoticed, while he becomes world famous for acts which are far less brilliant but more thrilling. This was the case with Kit Carson. The forty years of his mature life divide almost equally into two distinct halves. The first half was dominated by ruthless, reckless daring; the second, by considerate, thoughtful judgment.

Kit's training for the mountains had been by men who, like Old Gabe Bridger, were "a-goin' to show them Injun varmints who this here country belongs to." They had no regard for the rights of the Indians to their ancestral hunting grounds. Indians trying to protect their homelands were not looked upon as human beings, but as wolves that must be killed so as to make the mountains safe for the white man. The sooner they were put under, the sooner the mountains would be safe.

Kit admired these trapper leaders for their ruthlessness, daring and skill. He learned rapidly, believed as they believed, and outdid them in all three respects.

During his years with Frémont, Kit became acquainted and made friends with educated, thoughtful,

social-minded leaders. Just as he had admired the outstanding qualities of the mountain leaders, he admired
the outstanding qualities of these leaders of civiliza-
tion. Gradually he came to believe as they believed, to
place human rights above ruthless greed, and thoughtful judgment above reckless daring. In speech he always remained the ignorant backwoodsman. But as the
strength of his body declined, his wisdom and understanding increased remarkably.

During his seven years as Indian Agent, he was much
more concerned with the injustices being done Indians
by the whites than with the sins of the Indians. Often
he risked his position by trying to correct these abuses
and insisting that reservations of good farm land must
be set aside for these first Americans.

Where highly trained Regular Army generals had
failed against the Navajos, Kit, through wisdom and
understanding, conquered them with the loss of less
than a hundred lives. This same wisdom and understanding made him the only successful leader of volunteer New Mexican troops. During the Civil War, his
influence with the mountain tribes quite possibly
avoided a united uprising of the Indians west of the
Missouri. If it had taken place, it would have been
necessary for the Union to withdraw large forces of
soldiers from the battle lines, and the result might have
been disastrous. He would only go against the plains
Indians in the Battle of Adobe Walls after every hope

of peaceful treaty had been ruined by red tape and delays. And no other man ever made as many lasting treaties of friendship with the American Indians as Kit Carson.

Kit's influence over the mountain Indians, his conquering of the Navajos, his superb generalship in the Battle of Adobe Walls, and his Indian friendship treaties should, in times of peace, have won him a hero's place in American history. But with the nation divided by civil war, his most brilliant achievements were far overshadowed by greater, history-making events. Dozens of books and dime novels have been written about the reckless, daring adventures of Kit Carson's youth. Little has been told of the wisdom and greatness of his later years.

Though Kit had called Taos home for nearly forty years, he did not move his family back there when he was mustered out of the service. Fort Lyons had been built near the site of Bent's old trading post, and there was an army doctor at the Fort. Josefa was anxious that Kit be where the doctor could take care of him through the winter, so they moved into a little cabin a few miles from the fort. In the spring, she was going to have another baby and, after it was born, they would move to their own home in Taos.

Within three months after Kit left Fort Garland, the Ute unrest flared up again. This time the Commissioner of Indian Affairs thought it would be best if a delegation of Ute chiefs was brought to Washington for the making of a new treaty. In February, 1868, the Utes were invited to Washington to voice their complaints, and Kit was urged to come with them. He was now constantly troubled with bleeding from the throat, and did not think he could live if he tried to make the long stagecoach trip across the winter prairies. Both the Utes and the Commissioner were afraid the treaty would fail unless Kit was at the meeting, and urged him to go. Again Kit put the best interests of the United States and "Father Kit's Utes" ahead of his own interests, and took the stage down the Santa Fe Trail for the last time.

The treaty was successfully made and, at the end of March, Kit had got as far toward home as Denver. After several days in bed there, he took a stagecoach for La Junta, near Fort Lyons. Though the coming baby was due any day, Josefa met Kit at La Junta and took him home to their little cabin. On April 13th, little Josefita was born, but Josefa never regained her strength, and on April 23rd, she died of fever.

Kit's interest in living passed with Josefa. For more than twenty-five years he had looked forward to the time when he and this beautiful child whom he loved— for Josefa always remained a child to Kit—should be able to settle down and raise their family in peace. During all those years, there had been only a few scattered months when he had not been away from her in the service of his country. And now, when that service was finished, Josefa had been taken away.

All his life, Kit Carson had fearlessly crossed new and unknown frontiers. The old West was gone; the trackless mountains that he had loved as a trapper were now threaded with well-known caravan routes, and a railroad was nearly completed to the Pacific Coast. For Kit, there was no longer an unknown frontier—except the one Josefa had crossed. Patiently, he waited at Fort Lyons for the time when he might make his own crossing. It came just a month to the day after Josefa's.

On May 23rd, 1868, Kit sat listening to an old friend retell a story of the early days in the mountains. At the end of the story, Kit turned toward his friend. *"Adios, compadre,"* he whispered. "So long, my friend." And he crossed the pass to the new frontier.

Index

Adobe Walls (Battle of), 153–68, 173
Agua Caliente Valley, 126
American Fur Company, 38
Apache Indians, 23, 25–26, 136, 154–55, 160–62, 170
Arkansas River, 49, 100, 117, 136
Arapaho Indians, 67–69, 136, 154, 170
Ashley, General, 6–7, 35, 45
Astor, John Jacob, 38

Beale, Lieutenant, 131–32
Bear, grizzly, 64–66
Bear River, 42, 44
Beaubien, Carlos, 136
Beaver, trapping, 6–7, 9, 38–42
Beaver trade, 89
Beckworth, Jim, 7
Bent, Charles, 10, 12–15, 49–51, 89, 135
Bent, William, 50, 89, 154
Benton, Thomas Hart, 101–02, 108
Bent's Fort, 89
Big Snake River, 80
Black Whiteman (Cheyenne Indian), 50–54
Blackfoot Indians, 62–64, 76–80
Blue River, 57

Blunt, James G., 155
Boone, Daniel, 5
Boone Trail, 5, 8
Bridger, Jim, 7, 35, 59, 62, 75, 172
Broadus, Andy, 15–16
Brummel, George (Beau), 7
Buffalo, 83, 89

California, 26–29, 120–23
Californios, 127–32
Canadian River, 156–57
Canyon de Chelly, 148–51
Carleton, General, 155
Carson, Adaline, 84, 88–89, 97–98, 106, 138
Carson, Kit:
  ambition, 8, 9, 33
  appearance, 8
  Army service, 133, 172
  bear, encounter with, 64–66
  Bent, Charles, friendship, 15
  birth, 4
  brothers, see Carson, Mose; Carson, William
  caution, 103
  Cheyennes, Little Chief of, 54
  Civil War participation, 144, 173
  courage, 14, 21, 24–25, 29
  daughter, see Carson, Adaline